Encore

Living Your Life's Legacy

Contents

Forward

Nobody Gets Out of Here Alive

In my career, I've have led projects on digital health, consulted with family members processing tough news about the declining health of their loved one, and contributed to a number of books on healthcare IT and medical ethics. I now spend my days treasuring life's simple pleasures. My career as a physician has been a rich and rewarding one, so as I started to think about retirement, I leaned into the experience and expertise of other colleagues and friends who'd already made this transition. They helped me prepare for the initial period of mild disorientation that comes without the structure of work. Like it does for many, this period lasted several months. Then gradually, new routines set in, like going to the gym that grounds my day and taking up painting which adds a creative feel to my life. Because I was warned ahead of time about this transitional period, I learned to give myself time to sort it out. To let life sort itself out, to some extent. A book like Encore would have helped me immensely.

My husband and I talked a lot about our retirement as we made this transition. Instinctively, we dove into many topics covered in the book, focusing initially on money to make sure retirement at that time was even an option. We wanted to address all our concerns and possible scenarios. To know that much like physical health, facts can conquer fear. We hired a new financial management firm to help us sort out all of our finances and retirement options, and that firm connected us with a great new accountant for taxes. I changed out all our insurance, changed our investments, rethought our will, shut down my consulting business, cancelled my malpractice insurance, and signed up to work at a clinic for the uninsured as a volunteer. We made a plan, then we worked the plan.

We also tackled our home environment, using an app called Remember the Milk to track and schedule our tasks, to get rid of things we no longer needed, and to create a space where we could each feel comfortable enjoying both our individual and shared activities. While I had a home office, I was used to leaving daily to work at clinics, an office, or with teams. It took some time for both my husband and me to get accustomed to being in the house at the same time for long periods, and to navigate our respective needs for quiet and connection, as well as for stimulation and reflection. Changing our environment together paved the way for us to successfully move through this adjustment period.

Encore provides the structure, space, and helpful tools to address other parts of retirement and sparked other ideas for us to explore. Joy, which was something I didn't focus on as much when I was busy with my professional responsibilities, has bubbled to the top. As a way to combat the chronic pain I experience from a car accident many years ago, I took up belly dancing while I was still working. Now I'm part of a group of dancers who create our vibrant costumes together, dance at special events, and support each other as we continue to build our craft. This has been a source of connection and pride that I continue to savor in retirement, and gives me incentive to go to the gym, building the strength and stamina I need to perform. I'm very lucky to have found something that provides me joy and facilitates my physical, mental, and spiritual health.

Legacy is something I think about differently now. It actually surprises me how quickly I've moved away, psychologically and emotionally, from the world of death and dying. I was all in; now I'm all out. It feels sweet to respond to daily life through a more balanced lens. I was going to say *superficial*, but it's not that. It's just not seeing people in line at the grocery store and thinking about how we're all dying. I think about my legacy now as more about helping myself and others enjoy each and every moment, and being in the world in a way that increases good-will and kindness.

It's been interesting to witness how colleagues from my past like Hildy and Ann continue to touch my present and future. This book reflects many of the tools we used in collaboration on various business challenges, so to see them cleverly repurposed and organized to support others on their journey through retirement to end of life is a gift that keeps on giving. My hope is that you can benefit from some of these ideas to deepen the joy in your *Encore years.*

– Kate Christensen, MD Martinez, CA 2018

Note from the Authors

We met as accomplished businesswomen: steeped in process, business best practices, and the ability to galvanize diverse teams to create new ways of working. We support business professionals in various industries (healthcare, technology, and finance) in creating a shared vision, dealing with resistance to change, creating plans that sustain teams in times of doubt and despair, and practicing how to collaborate with others in times of change. At the center of everything is the need for people to manage their own change, when change is required. Each person on the team needs to feel heard and recognized for who they are, as well as for their unique contributions.

Whether at work, in a family, on a team, or even as part of a non-profit, we've facilitated people engaging with change in a way that honors their specific needs. We've taken these learnings and applied them to the changes we're each facing with aging, loss, and moving from one way of life to a new one. We're offering some tips and tools for those on a similar journey to provide comfort, perspective, and powerful choices.

It was hard to pretend big things weren't happening to our friends, our families, and our-selves as we age. We started talking and sharing our experiences. Clayton Christensen initially coined the term "Disruptive Innovation" to look at new value being created by displacing established beliefs and processes. In a moment of inspiration over coffee, we asked ourselves how we could apply "disruptive innovation" to the biggest transition of all: retirement and death. How could we help ourselves and others look at creating an "Encore" that we felt good about? Could we maintain a modicum of control through thoughtful planning, acceptance of the inevitable, and preparing for the unexpected?

We wanted to co-create the book we wished we'd access to in our times of need. We're turning the lens towards ourselves, to apply our learnings and research for your benefit. We've attended classes and workshops on death, dying, and hospice. We've read books and blogs, and we've researched how other cultures cope with their elderly and death. We've interviewed friends, colleagues, and strangers about their beliefs, dreams, and wishes, and we learn more everyday. We aren't *prescriptive*, but rather *descriptive* of what people are doing to prepare in all dimensions of their life for retirement to the end of life stage. We want to provide guidance to make these concepts easier to think about, talk about, and to experience the changes we need to make as we age.

– Hildy & Ann, Danville CA 2018

Why Us?

This book represents the collaboration of two women of the Baby Boomer generation who met and became friends while working in the healthcare industry. After watching colleagues and friends head towards retirement and deal with serious and life-threatening health concerns, we started to explore what our Encore looks like. We each had an interesting work and family life, but we both wondered: *What's next?*

As members of large families, we came together to share our stories of how we were coping—or not—with new daily challenges around the declining health and loss of our loved ones. We also listened deeply to the stories and confusion of others as they grappled with the theory—and reality—of mortality. We realized that while we're all on a similar journey, everyone tries to figure it out in "our own way" with little guidance or direction.

IV

Hildy's Background

Hildy is the middle of seven children in a large Irish-Catholic family. Her parents, Marge and John, had a loving relationship, and were married for over 50 years, before John passed away in 2001. Hildy has been married to Jim—her very best friend and college sweetheart—for over 35 years. They've raised three lovely children—Brennan, Katie, and Daniel—who are now out on their own, living their own lives.

Hildy holds an engineering degree from UC Berkeley, and MBA from St Mary's College. She first worked in Silicon Valley as a semiconductor design engineer, and later as management consultant on the human-centered design of software products and services. Hildy led two different consulting businesses for over 16 years and has experienced the rollercoaster of joy and stress that accompanies small business ownership.

In many ways, the last two years have been challenging for Hildy and her family. During surgery, Hildy's father-in-law James, passed away unexpectedly. Hildy's mother-in-law, Terry, was confronted with starting a new life. Hildy and Jim were there to help Terry with the transition. A year before, Hildy also welcomed her own 90-year-old mother, Marge, into her home. This involved selling Marge's home, the remodeling of Hildy's bedrooms to accommodate Marge's needs. Hildy spent 4 months helping Marge sort through what to take and what to give away. There was also the death of the mother of Hildy's close friend Dylia. Dylia's mother died peacefully in her arms, after several years of Dylia caring for her mother in her home. Witnessing Dylia's grief through that difficult time made Hildy realize she needed to be prepared for her own mother's death. There were even a few health scares with her siblings in recent years that had given Hildy pause. Hildy's brother, Brian, was diagnosed with a throat cancer that was treated successfully. Given his young age, it gave the entire family a glimpse their own mortality. Hildy's older brother, John, was also fitted for a pacemaker, and although he is healthy and fit, these types of procedures make you think. Given the new challenges, it became obvious that life wasn't going to continue on in the same way, leaving Hildy to wonder: *What can I do about all this?*

In discussing these issues with Ann, the seeds for this book were planted. Hildy and Ann set out to apply the techniques they'd used in their consulting work to the change going on in their lives. The intention was to learn, analyze and innovate their beliefs about aging and death by applying business tools they'd used in a fresh way—and also explore how to proactively prepare for the unknowns coming their way. Hildy and Ann decided that *retirement* is the wrong word for this next phase of life. Merriam Dictionary's definition of retirement means to "withdraw from action or danger," but instead, we prefer to think of retirement as a time to "engage in new adventures and learning." So, we're calling the retirement stage of life our *Encore*.

Ann's Background

Ann is the eldest of six children, born within eight years of each other. She vividly remembers taking care of her siblings, helping with the grocery shopping and cooking, and taking on responsibility for many things outside of her girlhood capabilities. Ann's mother was consistently overwhelmed, with a mercurial husband, who had trouble keeping a job and staying focused on the family.

Because of her formative family experiences, after marrying her beloved college sweetheart, Steve, Ann waited five years to have children. In Ann's marriage, she and her husband Steve, set their intentions to raise creative daughters, with a deep appreciation what it means to be a part of our global community. Today, their daughters, Lauren and Brooke are pursuing their dreams, and Ann shares some of their passions from stand-up comedy, to travel and writing.

As a well-intentioned working mother, Ann struggled with balance among all the needs and demands in her life. When a colonoscopy revealed several pre-cancerous polyps that had to be removed, Ann quickly developed a renewed appreciation for the power of self-care and community. She started playing water polo with a team of women who were committed to learning new things—a very physical game, one not typically associated with middle-aged women—each of whom offered unparalleled support to each other.

Ann had also been a consultant, helping innovation and technology teams around the world to convert their strategies into reality. Together, Hildy and Ann collaborated on projects to transform the way healthcare was provided and marketed through the implementation of digital tools and clinical support systems. They forged a bond and mutual appreciation for the similar, yet unique skills each of them brought to the table. They also shared their experiences as working mothers and faithful alumni of UC Berkeley.

Ann had always been fascinated with human nature, philosophy, and what makes the world "work" the way it does. She has a deep curiosity fueled by trying to decode a primary family filled with dysfunction and the intention *not* to repeat many of the patterns imprinted on her by parents who were trying to do their best, but were deeply challenged by life.

The desire to deepen the inquiry and learning led her to an integral coaching program in San Francisco offered by New Ventures West, which provided sophisticated frameworks and rigorous approaches to connect with others on their journey of change as they moved through their lives and careers. This coaching background and experience helped Ann facilitate numerous working sessions on everything from strategy development to launching new projects to dealing with dysfunctional teams, and more learning emerged around the complexities of relationships and living your mission.

Like many people, Hildy and Ann were caught up and in the busyness of their lives, so it'd been easy to push off even thinking about retirement and to totally ignore both the concept and reality of death. An unexpected brush with mortality and some deeply difficult personal losses stimulated Hildy and Ann's desire to think and talk about the inescapable truth—*no one gets out of here alive*. Ann witnessed this firsthand through a fellow yoga student at the studio where they both practiced—a surprising diagnosis of cancer of the appendix. Over a very short period of time, Ann watched a robust, healthy, 40-year-old father weaken, waste away, and finally die. How potent to witness the fragility of life—this encounter reawakened Ann's internal desire to learn more about how to live well and deeply in the face of aging and death.

Chapter 1

Introduction

Have you ever heard about a friend's terminal cancer diagnosis and wondered what it must be like for them to confront their imminent death?

Have you ever woken up in the middle of the night in a cold sweat worried if you'll have enough money for the rest of your life?

Have you ever attended a funeral and considered what people might say about you, after you're gone?

These are tough questions—but important ones. The unique way each of us deals with them is a complex reflection of how we were raised by our parents, our life experiences, our cultural norms around death, and our own primal fears about the process of dying and death. Rather than take this part of your journey alone, this playbook is intended to support you in exploring your hopes, dreams, fears, and planning for the final phase of life.

How might this next phase of your life be like the **Encore** of a fabulous artistic experience, where the positive energy and engagement with others creates a unique opportunity to extend the joy and deep connection with life? It's possible that being open-hearted and open-minded as you confront the aging and dying process is both a *practice* and a *promise of* developing deeper self-awareness and gratitude for the gift of life.

What's your Encore going to be? As the word *Encore* suggests, how can you revel in the stage of life that's *your* Encore? Our last phase of life *should* be as vibrant and engaging as every other stage of life that precedes it. The goal of this book is to help people redirect their fears about aging into positive energy for living in the now, and enjoying the ride. There's the wisdom of others to help you optimize your next phase of life and minimize your blind spots, as well as ideas and some tools to proactively address living life to your fullest capacity.

This is a book about transitions, not endings—the final transition each of us takes on our way out of the world of work and then out of this world—literally. Consider all the life transitions you've successfully navigated so far: teenager to independent adult, being single to marriage, parenthood, empty nests. We've learned a lot about how others cope with "expected" transitions as well as unexpected transitions like divorce, layoffs, moving to a new homes, cities, states, even different countries, and so on. There's no shortage of books, blogs, and resources available to support people with these transitions, but surprisingly, when it comes to retirement and death, there are fewer resources available, many of which are highly focused on only one specific aspect, (e.g., financial preparation for retirement or managing the details for a funeral service)—which is why this resource offers a more holistic, probing approach.

This playbook is a gift to yourself to imagine what this aging transition could feel like for you. Maybe you'll discover things about yourself that you never knew—like a passion for belly dancing, or the need to create a unique legacy. Feast on some food for thought, and savor the language and tools provided to navigate these transitions. The challenge to each of us as human beings is to enjoy the ride, while dealing with the life stages our Westernized culture loves to ignore: our own diminished capacities due to aging, illness, disability, and death.

The Baby Boomer generation has always tried to push the envelope in a quest to make our world a better place. Chances are, you've heard someone say, *"60 is the new 40!"*—it's no coincidence that Baby Boomers try to push the boundaries of what it means to remain relevant, look and feel great, and continue to make a positive difference in the world, using the wisdom they've gained from their life's experiences. While there's a desire to reject traditional cultural norms around the limitations imposed by aging, there are certain realities to confront when our bodies just won't cooperate in the same ways they did when we were younger, in our most peak form, fully able-bodied and usually without the threat of illness looming. Advances in medical technology and human genome research means that collectively, we're all living longer. The challenge of your Encore years, however, is not just to live *longer*, but to live *better*.

In dealing with their parents as they've aged, many Baby Boomers have had a sneak peek at what's in store for them—but still put off thoughts about their own lives and what lies ahead. Unfortunately, delayed planning for your Encore might result in limited options when the moment of truth arrives, or worse yet— lonely endings, with things left unsaid, undone, unresolved. To avoid those situations, this playbook offers **Resources, Stories, Bright Ideas,** and **Reflections** approaching all the possibilities available to you as you move into this next stage of life. An elderly friend we know commented, "There's a lot of lead in these Golden Years,"—so how might you look at ways to minimize the lead and maximize the gold for *yourself?*

Though this playbook was created with the specific considerations of older generations in mind, it's also a great resource for younger people to assess where they are, to reflect on their life, and to plan where they're going with courage and confidence as they age—after all, we never know when Death will come knocking, so it's best to try and keep your affairs in order, just in case. While aging is definitively a phenomenon defined by its physical manifestations, it's *also* a state of mind, and thus, easily influenced by the perceptions of others. Consider the very definition of aging, which in itself is continually changing. For example, the National Institutes of Health describes aging as, "... a decline or loss (de-tuning)," while the Minnesota Department of Health defines aging as the, "... development and maintenance of optimal mental, social and physical well-being and function in older adults." Aging is a unique, peculiarly individual experience that's directly affected by many subjective and objective factors.

Most people hate to think about aging and avoid discussing death because of the fear and grief associated with this stage of life and living. In the 1974 Pulitzer Prize book *The Denial of Death,* Ernest Becker identified the problem: "...[the] vital lie—man's refusal to accept his own mortality." Becker theorized that humans struggle to control our deep anxieties and go to great lengths to avoid the terror of death, by being, "bigger than life" and performing seemingly "immortal" feats— like waging war, or scaling mountains—to trick ourselves into thinking ourselves truly immortal. Recently, the front cover of *TIME* magazine led with the intriguing teaser,

"Can Google Solve Death?" profiling the launch of the Calico company, whose mission is to look at ways to extend and improve the quality of life for aging individuals and those living with severe disabilities. Unsurprisingly, the quest to tame death continues.

If you're reading this book, chances are, you're thinking about the next stage of life— maybe for yourself, or maybe for a loved one. Even amongst the closest of friends, this isn't an easy subject to broach. But harder still: seeing your parents age, experiencing your own aging or diminished capacity due to illness or an accident, without having the information and resources to process these new experiences.

If you're a natural procrastinator, planning for your Encore isn't top on your list. It may be fear preventing you from looking critically at how you might live your fullest life or you may just be enjoying life so much that you can't contemplate its end. "I think the basic notion of procrastination as self-regulation failure is pretty clear," says Timothy Pychyl, of Canada's Carleton University. "You know what you ought to do and you're not able to bring yourself to do it. It's that gap between intention and action." This exploration of your Encore stage of life will hopefully help melt away your fears and provide you with the impetus for proactive decisions.

Philosopher (and frequent *Oprah* guest) Eckhart Tolle, author of the cultural phenomenon *The Power of Now* notes, "When you become comfortable with uncertainty, infinite possibilities open up in your life." That sense of time ticking away—coupled with the sense of not knowing what'll happen to *you*—can make this a weird, and sometimes scary, time to experience. While it's easy to obsess about physical changes, the emotional impact and spiritual challenges can be even more overwhelming—especially if there's no venue to explore them. Holistic Encore planning should reflect the unique needs and desires of the person, offering ways to maximize joy and minimize stress and worry. After "playing" with this playbook, you should have a clear action plan using the **Life Stage** tool to create the Encore you desire.

For those who've experienced the major life transition of parenthood, you know just how many support systems exist to support those transitions: birthing classes, prenatal exercise classes, "Mommy and Me" playgroups... the list goes on and on. Every new mother benefits from the cumulative knowledge shared in the birth stories of their sisters and friends—and there's no lack of parenting tips offered by family, friends, and even strangers. *Generational* knowledge becomes *collective* knowledge in this sharing. Just imagine how powerful it could be if we had more venues, rituals, and support systems in place to honor the transitions from work to retirement, and from life to death, ways of sharing that generational and cumulative knowledge that we've accrued about these equally life-changing transitions. So few resources exist as we experience the later-in-life transitions—even the old union "gold watch and retirement party" ritual has fallen by the wayside. With fewer resources available to navigate these transitions, where does that leave us?

Have you ever seen a "Death and Me" class? Do you know of any retirement midwives? These aren't the kinds of things you hear about everyday. And as many new retirees are discovering, leaving one kind of fulfilling life to begin another—*outside* of work—can be challenging. In a 2013 study performed by the UK Institute of Economic Affairs, it was reported that 40% of retirees suffer from clinical depression, while 6 out of 10 report a decline in health. It's believed that the underlying cause of this decline stems from the loss of tangible things offered in a workplace: relationships with colleagues, daily routines which don't require decision-making about what to do today, and the deep gratification which can occur when you're exposed to new ideas, people, and projects.

Humans are social creatures, and we learn from each other. The gift of sharing our stories, our worries, and our wishes can be a powerful balm. This playbook could be the catalyst for you to start your own conversations with your family, friends, or colleagues. You could also opt to join our online community to learn and share with others who want to explore some of the ideas from this book with other supportive people.

Encore is intended to help you look at how to live your best possible life through the exploration of more than just the financial planning that all retirees must contemplate. Through guided exercises and worksheets, you'll have an opportunity to reflect on topics such as what sparks joy for you as you age, your ideal environment for your later life, and methodologies for cultivating your existing connections, as well as ideas for how to create new connections. There'll be an opportunity to look at what constitutes a "good death" for you, the legacy you might want to leave, explorations of deeper levels to your spirituality, and the challenge to look at your health practices both now—and in the future.

Ann's Story

Recently, one of my colleagues, Sally, was diagnosed with stage 4 ovarian cancer. Although her friends knew she'd had chemo and was getting her head shaved, looking at her bald head over dinner was still a shock to their sensibilities. Imagine how Sally felt—walking into a restaurant full of presumably healthy people while her baldness clearly marked her as "different" (and therefore, potentially scary)—to everyone she encountered. At a time when she yearned for deeper connections to life and others, there was also an imperceptible "pulling away" from others, as she embodied the telltale signs of illness—and the possibility of impending death—in such a visible way.

Another friend, embarrassed by the condition, delayed going to her doctor for her persistent hemorrhoids. After four years of suffering silently, she finally went to her physician, had surgery for the condition, and was shocked that a biopsy indicated Stage 3 rectal cancer. According to research from the *World Journal of Gastroenterology*, statistics from Korea and Japan indicate colorectal cancer is the number one cause of cancer morbidity for women over 65. Women as a demographic may be more susceptible to this disease due to embarrassment, and are more likely to ignore warning signs for longer durations, have difficulties advocating for themselves with doctors, and doctors often dismiss women who present with symptoms that aren't as readily diagnosable than they would men. This anecdote and this data serves as a reminder that it's all-too-easy to deny the nagging awareness from our physicality that something *just isn't right,* and the consequences of ignoring early warning signs in your body can be profound.

Whatever the catalyst—it's a wake-up call, an indicator that there's more out there to consider than you'd previously wanted to think about. It's time to break down the powerful wall of denial about retirement and death that permeates our culture. Here's to you for picking up this book—manifesting the courage to confront your mortality with grace, dignity, and maybe even a touch of humor. In The Doors song "Five to One", Jim Morrison sings, "No one here gets out alive." With that in mind, we ask you this: How do you want to spend the time you've got left? ⊛

What This Book Does / Does Not Do

This Book Does:	This Book Does Not:
Provide resources to spur you to think about all the aspects of life's greatest transitions of all—retirement and death	Include an exhaustive set of legal documents, tools, and resources for anything you ever wanted to know about retirement or death but were afraid to ask.
Offer you the ability to jump to what you need or want to explore in a nonlinear fashion.	Require reading cover to cover to derive value.
Include places to record your thoughts, feelings, and insights for just you or to share with others when you're ready.	Shy away from an approach for dealing with what scares you about your own end of career and late-in-life life decisions, process, and realities.
Focus on the secular, while honoring spirituality.	Advocate specific religious traditions or belief systems.

Chapter 3

Encore Wheel and Your Life Stage

Your life is your canvas, and you are the masterpiece. There are a million ways to be kind, amazing, fabulous, creative, bold, and interesting.

- Kerli

The 8 sections in the **Wheel of Life** represent different aspects of your life in your retirement and/or Encore stage. Most often, people think about money and "bucket list" activities when they're planning for this stage of life. We have financial planners in midlife, career coaches for career advice, family and marriage counselors for middle-age issues—but we don't always have consultants for how to live well in the Golden Years.

There are 8 areas for you to consider as you plan your **Life Stage**. Reflect on how prepared you are right now for this next stage of life, and consider what areas need more time and attention. The center of the wheel is a rating of 0— meaning you haven't given much focus to that aspect of your life. For example, one person might overlook their living environment and therefore neglect environment issues. Their two-story family home might therefore become an obstacle if and when that person starts having issues climbing stairs. You might also consider that living in a home alone doesn't provide the social interaction you enjoyed when your family surrounded you. A single-story home, on the other hand, can provide options to age in place and remain independent. The chapter on environment will explore multiple living situations for your consideration.

Mini Wheel

The outer edge of the wheel is a rating of 5—plot a point here, if you're *completely satisfied* with your planning and preparation in this aspect of your Encore life. Maybe you've saved more than enough money, or you expect to inherit prior to your retirement stage. In that case, Money would be plotted as a 5 on the wheel, and you don't have to spend much energy focused on that aspect of your Encore plan.

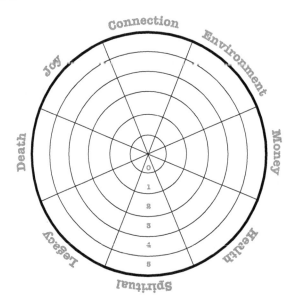

Now, by connecting all the dots you plotted in the 8 regions of the **Wheel of Life**, you can create the "baseline" outer edge of your wheel. The new perimeter of the circle represents where you are now in your **Wheel of Life** planning for your Encore. This can often look like a jagged wheel, incapable of supporting you as you're driving down the highway of life. Just being aware of this can lead to positive changes, often with an immediate impact. The wheel isn't a "one and done" activity— we encourage you to assess your wheel yearly, and make changes to your Life Stage plan to change your wheel shape.

Encore Wheel Evolution

Hildy's Wheel, August 2015

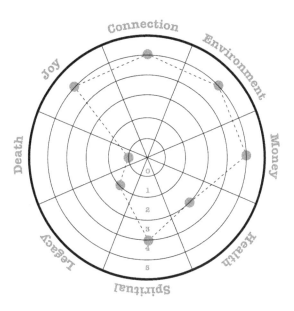

In 2014, Hildy took a break from work to help get her mother settled, and to deal with a serious bout of menopausal insomnia. In 2015, Hildy was focused on improving her health and thinking about what her Encore might look like. Hildy lost a significant amount of weight and by the end of 2016, was exercising on a regular basis. In December of 2016, she went back to work. The focus for 2017 was to ensure her joint retirement savings were secure—especially with the upcoming wedding of her only daughter. Being off work for a few years reduced Hildy's confidence on her family's retirement savings amount and one of her new goals, after revisiting her Wheel of Life is trying to figure out how to retire before the age of 67.

Hildy's Wheel, End of 2017

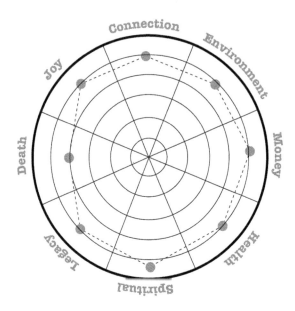

In Hildy's 2016 wheel—while her improvements to both her health and legacy were apparent—she still had some work to do. Based on her reassessment of her **Wheel of Life**, the next few years demonstrated that she should focus on spending more time considering what her retirement and optimal death might look like.

Ann's Wheel, August 2015

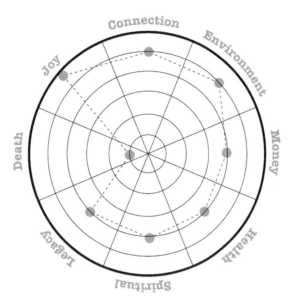

Ann's September 2015 **Wheel of Life** reflected the struggle she was having, trying to come to terms with her mother's death and the lack of emotional closure it had sparked for her. She also realized the importance of updating key financial documents, given that her children were now adults. Ann identified an advisor to help them through the Executor process up until age 40. She also decided to do a "household purge" and freshen up her home environment to reflect the life she was living now as an empty nester, rather than trying to hold onto the years of active mothering that she'd enjoyed so much. After some frustrating misinformation and a misdiagnosis, she finally found a physician who supported her in resetting her digestive track and successfully addressing her numerous food allergies. Subsequently, her health blossomed. Ann also started working with an energy healer, which she found to be a surprisingly gratifying experience.

Ann's Wheel, September 2016

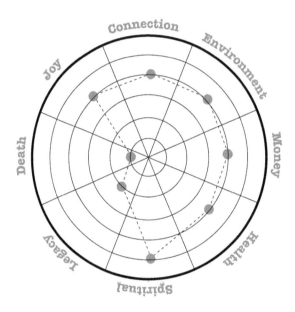

Ann's September 2016 **Wheel of Life** painted a much different picture. She and her husband decided to jointly tackle some deferred maintenance on both their home and garden. Ann also made a conscious decision to reduce the number of projects and clients with whom she was working to devote more time to writing and new endeavors that nourished her inquisitive nature. As you embark on the next phase of your journey and time seems to speed up, how bumpy does it look like your ride will be based upon your **Wheel of Life**? Ask yourself: Are there any things that jump out at you that you can start doing, stop doing, or amplify as you prepare for your Encore? If you had to draw a picture of your life now, what would it look like?

Encore Wheel and Life Stage Exercises

You can download our Encore exercise from our website at https://yourencoreteam.com/. You should plan on revising your wheel or life stage goals as you age and your priorities change.

Once you've completed the **Wheel of Life** exercise, the chapters of this book will help you think about what you might do to balance your wheel. For each section of the wheel, you can determine what actions you might take over the following year to move towards your overall Encore goals. The action plan you create can be captured in the **Life Stage** template, shown below. The purpose of the **Life Stage** is to have a one-page snapshot of your Top 3 To-Do's in the 8 areas of your life that make up your Encore plan.

You can refresh your plan to balance your wheel of life as your priorities and needs will change as you age. The **Life Stage** is a living document and we suggest you look at often to meet your goals of living your best Encore life.

Ann's

Joy	Connections	Health	Spirituality	Legacy
Write more	Interact with babies regularly	Complete healing of broken arm	Take a class @1440 University	Complete book of short stories
Play in nature every day	Take annual trip with kids and siblings	Get a baseline hearing test	Attend dharma talks	Review Dad's writings and share with family
Celebrate life		Try Pilates on a reformer		Be the change I want to feel within our extended family
	Environment		**Death**	
	Plant vegetable garden		Update electronic records	
	Repaint interior of home		Clean out basement and garage	
	Plant more natives			

Money			Bright Ideas	
Create workshops and other offerings to support Encore community			Go on weekly adventures	
			Explore a "she shed"	
Play with new business ideas			Live in another country for a month	

Stage Left · Center Stage · Stage Left

Ann's sample Life Stage exercise

Hildy's

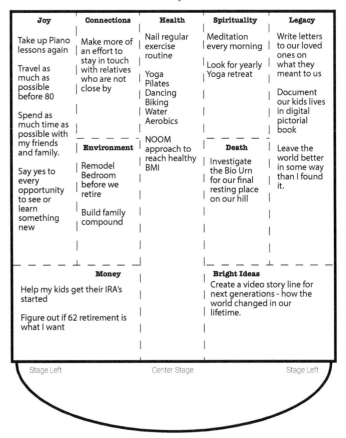

Joy	Connections	Health	Spirituality	Legacy
Take up Piano lessons again	Make more of an effort to stay in touch with relatives who are not close by	Nail regular exercise routine	Meditation every morning	Write letters to our loved ones on what they meant to us
Travel as much as possible before 80		Yoga Pilates Dancing Biking Water Aerobics	Look for yearly Yoga retreat	Document our kids lives in digital pictorial book
Spend as much time as possible with my friends and family.		NOOM approach to reach healthy BMI		
Say yes to every opportunity to see or learn something new	**Environment** Remodel Bedroom before we retire		**Death** Investigate the Bio Urn for our final resting place on our hill	Leave the world better in some way than I found it.
	Build family compound			

	Money		Bright Ideas	
Help my kids get their IRA's started			Create a video story line for next generations - how the world changed in our lifetime.	
Figure out if 62 retirement is what I want				

Stage Left · Center Stage · Stage Left

Hildy's sample Life Stage exercise

Chapter 2

How To "Play" With This Play- book

What matters is that by shifting your focus to appreciation, you slow down your survival mechanism. Love, joy and giving will all trigger the same positive transformation.

– Tony Robbins

It might sound funny that we use the word *fun* and ask you to *play* with new ideas and learnings in a book focused on dying and death. Consider the fact that children immediately reach out in curiosity—with a spirit of inquiry—to explore what they don't know using all their senses. Consider your natural processing style—the sense you lean on most naturally when learning. If you prefer to read or write down information to process, your dominant processing style is most likely *visual*. Do you need to talk through your thinking process? If so, chances are you're primarily an *aural* or *auditory* processor. If you're the kind of person who likes to get in there and "do it yourself" to learn something new or figure out how something works, then you're most likely a *kinesthetic* processor.

Whatever your natural processing style, you can use this book as a reference, a journal, or a compassionate guide to helping yourself and loved ones deal with the great unknowns of life.

Sprinkled throughout the book are **Personal Stories**, curated **Digital Resources** links, **Bright Ideas** to help you explore a particular topic, and **Reflection** questions for you to consider, as you move through each section of the book.

Personal Stories are from one of the authors' experiences, or are the summarization of stories that have come from their friends or family, often with names changed to protect the privacy of people generous enough to share these stories. Because humans are natural connectors, stories are a great way to remember insights based on the experience and wisdom of others—a way of passing down generational or cumulative knowledge. The key is finding something that you can relate to your own life and personal journey. You're also invited to contribute your personal stories and connect with others and us. Consider the **Personal Stories** collected throughout Encore to be like Case Studies—some of them may feel familiar, and others may demonstrate things that you've never thought about before. As the saying goes, "Your mileage may vary!" ☸

Digital Resources and the exercises in each section of the book can be found on our website at www.yourencoreteam.com. The **Digital Resource PDF** contains links to additional online content that Ann and Hildy found in their research for this book e.g. "How much do I need to save for retirement?" or "Where can I get a POLST (Physician Orders Life-Sustaining Treatment) form?" Keep in mind that the internet is an ever-evolving entity—while we've tried to keep these links as up-to-date as possible through regular audits of the supplementary **Digital Resources PDF**, it's entirely possible that in-between our audits, some of these sites may change URL or "go dark." If you encounter a 404 Error along the way, feel free to reach out to us at www.yourencoreteam.com to alert us, so we can make sure that we update the document for you and for future users. If the information is something you need immediately, we recommend performing a web search on the title, author, or keywords.

 **Bright Ideas** are suggested actions you can implement to explore a topic. While many of us can read an article or blog and immediately put its key ideas into practice, some people prefer the structure and support of specific tools and guideds to practice incorporating new ideas into their daily lives. **Bright Ideas** might include ways for you to expand your repertoire of coping skills, and what importance that has in your own unique journey. **Bright Ideas** can also help you translate a new idea or concept into reality for you and your unique situation—think of the **Bright Ideas** as "jumping off" points, where you can translate something from theory into practice, or figure out how to put your own personal "spin" onto things.

 The **Reflections** journal is an invitation to record your unarticulated dreams, fears, wishes, and hopes as you make your own transition or help a family member make theirs. Recording your thoughts, feelings, fears, hopes, and ideas will facilitate self-reflection— without judgment—when you encounter your deep-seated fears or even challenge some of your life-long assumptions.

Resistance – What Might You Encounter?

Bringing up the topics of death, dying, or aging isn't going make you most popular person at a party—trust us, we tried. Surprisingly, nobody was having it. When people get together to celebrate, they want to connect to and exult in life—they don't want to talk about it ending! Between the two of us, we experienced the whole spectrum of people's emotions: from dark humor to outright disgust, and everything in-between. Keep in mind that everyone is on their own journey—sometimes your friends and family won't be able to meet you at the point you're at in yours—and that's okay.

Aging is easier to discuss as a *general* concept—but once you touch on end-of-life planning by getting into the *specifics* of what an "ideal death" looks like and feels like, things can go downhill—and fast. Consider all the familial, cultural, spiritual, generational, and community imprinting that starts even before our understanding of mortality clicks in. Some families talk about death as a part of living and being human, openly encouraging dialogues that explore the mystery of death, while others eschew the very *mention* of human mortality. Even clinicians— the very people to whom we entrust our lives and health—can be hesitant to broach the subject with their patients. "We talk about personal medicine, but there should be personalized death too," said Dr. Dilip Jeste, director of UC San Diego School of Medicine's Sam and Rose Stein Institute for Research on Aging. "Finding out what kind of death a person would like to have shouldn't be a taboo topic." Dr. Dilip reviewed over 20 years of research on this subject—finding only 36 pertinent articles to help guide a whole world's worth of people through aging and dying.

According to expert citations in Virginia Hughes' *National Geographic Magazine* feature, "Only Human", understanding death develops over the following stages for children:

Stage	Age
Understanding death's irreversibility	Typically between 4-5 years of age
Understanding death's non-functionality	Typically between ages 5-7 years of age
Understanding death's universality	Typically age 7 and beyond; sometimes this takes a lifetime to understand

Hildy's Story

Throughout the course of researching this book, I brought up the subjects of retirement and death planning in a variety of social settings—I was curious to see the how different cross-sections of my own life felt about these issues, and how they navigated talking about them in a setting where it wasn't a crisis requiring action. As human nature varies, so did the reactions I received— but as I'd suspected, there was a pattern. First, there was the gentle teasing of discomfort: "What a *great* topic for dinner, Hildy!" Or a more extreme reaction, a good friend simply said, "I'm sorry, Hildy, but I can't talk about this without crying or getting really upset", and unexpectedly shut me down.

I grew accustomed to fits of nervous laughter, when I tried to share some of the research I'd been doing, like when I attended a Death Café, which is a group of interested people who come together to explore their questions about end of life realities, listening to other people's experiences with death. These events are organized throughout the world, so chances are, if you're curious, there's probably one in your area. Death Cafés usually have a moderator who sets up the evening and checks in with the small groups after their conversation, but the events themselves tend to be unstructured by design, with the intent of giving a people a safe space to share their thoughts and feelings about death. There are many internet-based groups where you can engage in a social discussion online, if you're unable or reluctant to meet up in person to discuss such a loaded topic. ✸

Although intellectually we may understand that we can't "wish away" aging and eventually death by pretending they don't exist, we can—and do—change the subject, shudder in dismay, or even get mad at the person who raises the subject. While arguably, these reactions aren't as extreme as *thanatophobia* (the clinical fear of dying), these reactions to the reality of death are common. You can't control everything that happens to you in your life—we all know this, rationally. But you can control how you *react to* and *plan for* your death—think of it like preparing for a natural disaster, like an earthquake, except you've got a lot more lead time. While no amount of preventive actions will stop death, what it *can* do is to relieve some of intense emotional reactions and stresses, as your mortality approaches. This is exactly why emergency teams run drills with various contingencies—so they'll be calm in the face of real crisis. Likewise, by addressing your fears in the *present* and *planning* for possible coping mechanisms and contingencies, you can reduce some of the anxiety and stress associated with death.

Resistance can be a teacher for us—it alerts us to blind spots, the filters we'd rather embrace than to question them or make changes. An example of a *blind* spot is a person's inability to see that being in a social setting causes them to speak faster and louder—while a *filter* is a way of viewing the world based upon your upbringing, education, age, or other situational factors. An example of a *filter* would be assuming that all people are just like us and love talking about intense, emotionally-charged topics. Death is one such topic—many of us can't bear to confront the thought of everything they know and love ending. Regardless of your blind spots, filters, or resistance—you're not alone. And this book shows that ready or not, you've taken one of the biggest first steps forward—kudos to you!

Some of us hold internalized superstitions: that even thinking or talking about death will bring it on swifter. Still others want to explore this greatest of unknowns. There's a variety of books available to the curious, all centered on death and dying, therapists who specialize in supporting people in exploring these issues, and spiritual guides, shamans, and other enlightened figures who bring a deep appreciation for cultural traditions outside of the Westernized approach to the world, each of whom help to explore the connections between birth and death, human nature, and the mother nature.

We've all heard stories of people who have had a near-death encounter, stories of people who "saw the light" and came back again, giving many people hope that there's something that comes next. Through Western religious traditions and in popular culture, this idea is *universally held*, but not necessarily *universally believed*. In the book, *The Violet Hour: Great Writers at the End*, author Kate Rope compiles fascinating vignettes about how many canonical writers embraced their mortality. Likewise, many of our most insightful artists find the great frontier of death perplexing, worthy of study after study in its exploration. We can also learn from clinicians and caregivers who deal with death daily, such as the Zen Hospice Project in San Francisco. This non-profit organization offers hands-on care to the dying—as well as inspiring research efforts supported by thought leaders from companies like IDEO and organizations like TED. Zen House is always accepting volunteers open to the frank discussion of death, to offer support to the dying, and actively seeks out clinicians who want to focus on end-of-life care. In a recent *San Francisco Chronicle* feature on Maurice Ruark, a hospice nurse who worked in San Francisco's underserved

Tenderloin district for over 27 years, Ruark noted that despite its challenges, it was the best job he ever had, because he'd learned how to live from those who were dying. ✵

> *Our mission is to help change the experience of dying. We create a space for living that offers the opportunity for individuals, their loved ones and caregivers to find comfort, connection, and healing in this shared human experience. Through our pioneering model of care, we inspire each other to live fully.*

—Zen Hospice Project mission statement

Hildy's Story

While researching this book, Padma—an Indian friend of mine—told me her mother wouldn't tolerate any discussion of death or dying. Her mother went into a deep depression after the loss of her parents, and couldn't deal with any discussions of death, even in the abstract. This makes it very difficult for Padma to figure out her mother's end-of-life wishes. While many medical professionals encourage the use of a Do Not Resuscitate (DNR) form for aging patients, in Padma's family, they can't even discuss the possibility of a need for a DNR form. Padma will need to make a lot of critical decisions—while she's grieving, and without the benefit of her mother's guidance or knowledge of her specific wishes.

You've already crossed a significant chasm in picking up this book. Maybe your feelings about death show up in more subtle ways. Pay attention to when you feel a resistance creeping into a desire to turn the page, put the book down, or get rid of it altogether. There's a Buddhist saying: "What we resist—persists." Stay the course. Stick with the book.

If you ever experience these feelings when thinking about your own Encore years and death—or if you're prone to panic attacks or other physical manifestations of anxiety—we suggest you employ some simple meditations, or to use breathing exercises to reduce stress. ✵

Bright Idea

This breathing exercise can be a great anxiety and stress-reducer, and also helps if you have trouble sleeping at night due to persistent, recurrent thoughts.

This breathing exercise is a 4-8-7 breathing technique, which you can do quietly perform while sitting or lying down anywhere. Breathe in as deeply as you can through your nose while counting to 4, filling your lungs to their maximum capacity. Hold your breath, while counting to 8. Finally, release the breath noisily through your mouth to the count of 7, expelling all air from your lungs completely. Repeat these steps 3-6 times, or until you feel yourself returning to your natural baseline.

For those of us who've derived much of our self-worth from work, retirement can feel like a kind of death. Leaving the world of work can *feel* like the death of the person we used to be, without a clear image of who will replace that version of ourselves. For others—who've been out of the working world for a while—thinking about and learning the curve of the next big life events can feel scary, like something we'd rather put off until later—much, much later. In our experience, we've found that *tools* can help pierce resistance to talking about retirement, aging, and death. So we've applied our combined years of professional experience with strategy, innovation, process design, group facilitation and coaching to develop practical, actionable tools paired with key context to help you think through 8 areas on your **Wheel of Life**, ranging from how to cultivate joy to managing your legacy.

The key tool is our **Wheel of Life**, comprised of 8 sections which you can work through to create an actionable plan that works for you and supports you on your unique personal journey. We call this actionable plan your **Life Stage** map, to help you chart your own Encore.

The **Life Stage** has space for your top take-away from each chapter of the book. Your **Life Stage** can and should evolve over time. This isn't a one-time activity—we advise you to write the date on your map and revisit it as needed. Your life circumstances will change as you age, depending on your circumstances. There are always marriages, divorces, births, deaths, and illnesses that visit every family, all of which change the landscape of your present—and your future. Your health could abruptly change your plans. Or, you could fall in love, join a new community, start a philanthropy, or even win the lottery—so what would you do then? Like any canvas, you start out with the bare bones, adding layers to it as time passes. You're the artist, and your **Life Stage** is an extension of the art of all the living you've already done, reflecting your unique sensibilities, beliefs, and passion. As Leonardo Da Vinci famously said, "Art is never done, only abandoned!"

Resistance-O-Meter Exercise

You can download Encore exercise from our website at

https://yourencoreteam.com/.

Rate your resistance to discussing your retirement and death

(and that of others, if you wish) using the following tool. Remember to

date it, as it can be used a baseline to see if and when things change for you or others.

You: Plot a Triangle

Significant Others: Plot Diamonds

Your Parents: Plot Squares

Your Children: Plot Hearts

No Discussion   **Freely Discuss Death**

Sample

Chapter 4

Self-Reflection

To know yourself as the Being underneath the thinker, the stillness underneath the mental noise, the love and joy underneath the pain, is freedom, salvation, enlightenment.

—Eckhart Tolle

One of the most interesting things about aging is the subtle and surprising shift that can occur when your perceptions of your own hard-earned knowledge and mastery of a subject aren't really the wisdom you need. The sense of what we know can be suddenly replaced by a shocking awareness of how little you actually know. Human biorhythms change over time, and unlike in our younger years—where we could often power through tons of "to do's" when we needed to get things done with little or no sleep—these tactics may not work as your energy levels drop and sleeping patterns change. Your strategies for dealing with difficult colleagues in the workplace might not be effective in the home, when dealing with aging parents or siblings. You may think you have all the time in the world, but no one knows exactly how much time they have—so it's all about making the best of whatever you've got.

It can be helpful to approach your Encore phase with a fresh perspective and a keen sense of humor. Vivian Clayton—a geriatric neuropsychologist who has performed research on wisdom since the 1970s—learned that people considered wise tend to be good decision makers, and the 3 key components of wisdom are *cognition, reflection,* and *compassion*. What's interesting about this is the lack of *explicit knowledge* or *mastery* of a given topic as a key ingredient of wisdom. It appears the gift of *reflection* vs. *acting* on previous experience as a basis for moving forward and making decisions in your Encore period grows in importance.

With all the adages about the wisdom of the aged, there are definitely some pearls to be harvested. You can help locate those pearls most precious to you by stepping back from your life, reflecting with eyes and heart wide open, and deciding how you might want to proceed. It'll also help you to make more conscious and hopefully better decisions when confronting an "age spurt", or a loss. An "age spurt" can be a physical manifestation of aging like a wrinkle or sagging jowl line or forgetting a dear friend's name or needing reader eyeglasses when your vision used to be "perfect."

A shift in focus from the external, *thinking* way of learning to a more internally-focused exploration on how *feeling* your way through to live well as you age can be simultaneously disconcerting and liberating. The shift occurs in your Encore phase, because you suddenly have time to reflect on yourself that you didn't have in your busier, younger years. In the Berlin Wisdom Project—a comprehensive study on wisdom—a clear distinction was made between general wisdom, where you can process life from an observer's point of view to a more nuanced, personal wisdom view which is based upon plumbing the insights of your own life. In the book, *Sailing Home*, Norman Fischer equates the journey of late adulthood to that of the adventures of Ulysses, trying his best to return to home and his metaphysical self after the trials and tribulations he's encountered in the world. Using the tools in this book is like Ulysses, using the challenges to better understand who he's become on his hero's journey through life.

Think of the many things that throughout your life have demanded your time, your energy and your love. From spouses and children to siblings and jobs and your community—each day has demanded so much of you. Patterns of habituation have built up over the years, and these can become difficult to see, much less to penetrate. Reflection is often marginalized or relegated to brief moments between activities. One of the unfortunate downfalls to Westernized society is that we're more comfortable as *Human Doings* instead of *Human Beings*.

Unstructured retirement can lead to depression and resentfulness when you can no longer perform at previous levels. In his book *How to Retire Happy, Healthy, and Free*, Ernie Zelinski said all of us need 3 basic things for a successful retirement: *purpose, structure, and community.*

Despite the fantasy that we'll luxuriate in a slower paced life with no demands upon us, that's the exact opposite of what most of us need in retirement.

Where Are You in The Game of Life...And Aging?

Looking objectively at yourself and harnessing the power of information to prepare for the changes engendered by aging can help us feel in control and embrace the surprises coming our way. In retirement, you actually have time to focus on yourself. *What areas will you explore? What are your options?*

Gail Sheehy, author of *Passages*, has discovered in her studies that people who ground their remaining years to passion are more likely to build new interests and lives that are both satisfying and rewarding. She advocates taking the "time flies" test if you aren't sure what your passion might be. *What are you doing when you're fully engaged with it, and don't even realize that hours have gone by? What did you love to do when you were young and unencumbered by responsibility?*

AARP has online resources, subscription services, and reports for you to use to benchmark yourself, and they often publish interesting research articles like "The Happiness Report," based on research geared to better understand what happiness and well-being meant to middle-aged and older Americans, with the objective of developing benefits to increase happiness and well-being among its constituents. The report demonstrates that much of person's happiness centers on 2 significant areas, both of which are in your control. The happiest people have good relationships and good health—the latter of which, admittedly, isn't *totally* under your control. Connection and mobility are also keys to a fruitful Encore, and people with partial or full disabilities can seek or create opportunities to connect via Internet or telephonic meetups or classes.

AARP also published the report, "What to Expect When You're Expecting to Turn 50...60...70..." Much like the "What to Expect When You're Expecting" guides for new parents, AARP's guide helps new retirees navigate what kind of physical and emotional changes to expect in during the Encore years. Below is a list to consider paying attention to as your age.

What to Expect in Your 50s, 60s and 70s

- Save your skin
- Preserve Your Senses
- Motivate Your Metabolism
- Bone Up for Good Health
- Keep Your Heart Stong
- Improve Your Sex Life
- Ramp Up Your Immunity
- Take Fewer "Nighttime" Trips
- Be Happy
- Stay Sharp

Ann's Story

As I got closer to my 50th birthday, things started happening with my body that I hadn't anticipated and certainly didn't welcome. I felt lethargic, overweight, and flabby, and didn't know what to do. A friend asked if I wanted to join her at a Masters water polo practice at a local women's college. While I'd been on the first women's water polo team at UC Berkeley for a quarter and a strong swimmer, I was totally unprepared and terrified to even show up.

I was so out of shape that the bottoms of my feet tingled, and I swam over both my conditioning and ability levels. I persevered, however, and am now a proud member of the Soda Mom's Water Polo team. The gift of getting in better shape by reconnecting with a dormant passion has been eclipsed by the joy, camaraderie, and mutual support we offer each other through menopause, loss, and life. Here's to finding your passion—and going for it! ✸

Journal Reflections

To support your exploration of where you are in the game of life and to help you achieve a balance with your precious time, we're including **Reflection** points throughout the book. We invite you to help yourself to greater self-awareness about what you need as you experience the sometimes-scary but also sometimes exhilarating experiences of retiring, aging, and dying.

In a recent HuffPo blog, the author noted the benefits of physically writing vs. typing your thoughts are threefold: the ability to see the physical paper in front of you, motor stimulation by using your hand, and engaging in the cognitive task of remembering what the letters looks like and then recording them. Also, given that journaling is a reflective activity, surprises often emerge as we connect our heart and head and write about what we're thinking. You have the power of choice to pick among these open-ended questions and to use them as a way to record snapshots in time, mark your progress or your fears, and celebrate your personal triumphs or takeaways. Over time, you can also look back at previous journals and observe—without judgment—patterns and therefore gain subtle but important insights. Committed journalers might notice their days are much happier if they start the day with quiet time to reflect and journal vs. jumping right into activities, even when under time pressure.

Given the plethora of ways to capture, codify, and process information today, a great opportunity for building self-awareness and deep engagement with the larger issues of living, retiring, and dying is often overlooked. A daily practice of reflection in the morning to set your intentions for the day and then reflect on the lessons learned at the end of the day is a powerful tool. Not only is the physical act of getting things out of your head and onto paper important; it also fosters personal accountability around making and keeping commitments to yourself. Boosting the impact of reflection is the ability to put pen to paper, connecting mind, body, and spirit through the physical act of translating thoughts and feelings into tangible words on paper.

For some of us, looking at a blank piece of paper in a journal is intimidating and harkens back to trying to crank out a research paper for school. Throughout this book, we offer relevant prompts to help you think and feel your way to greater clarity about some of these thorny issues. These questions will help you look at where you are now in your life and make some fresh connections with yourself and maybe others by discussing your answers. Feel free to pick and choose among the questions, but again, learn as you observe yourself—again, without judgment—selecting which questions you want to answer and which ones you decide to reject. You're giving yourself a very precious gift, which can enrich your **Life Stage**.

 **Self Reflection**

How would you describe yourself at this point in your life journey?

_____

_____

_____

_____

_____

How do you take care of yourself?

_____

_____

_____

_____

What nourishes you?

_____

_____

_____

_____

_____

What do you know about your inner world? (Thoughts, feelings, emotions)?

_____

_____

_____

_____

_____

_____

What are primary sources of meaning in your life?

_____

_____

_____

_____

_____

_____

Self in Relationship to Others

How would others describe you?

_____

_____

_____

_____

_____

How are you taking care of your relationships?

_____

_____

_____

_____

_____

What relationships are toxic for you? Nourishing for you?

_____

_____

_____

_____

_____

Who's in your network of support, and how might you lean into others for help?

_____

_____

_____

_____

How and when do you reach out for support? Are you your own "best friend?"

_____

_____

_____

_____

_____

 **Observations**

What was it like to answer these questions?

_____

_____

_____

_____

_____

Which questions did you embrace and which did you resist?

_____

_____

_____

_____

_____

Why? Any insights you can put into action after doing this?

_____

_____

_____

_____

_____

Take time to re-read these reflection questions and your answers to them, as they might change as you age and different parts of your life change as well.

Bright Idea

These questions and their answers can also be used to create a "Legacy Book" for you or as a gift. Buy a blank journal and put a set of specific questions at the top of each page to stimulate your heart, head,

and what you might want to share with your family as a tangible gift for

the next generation.

Chapter 5

Joy

Focus on the journey, not the destination. Joy is found not in finishing an activity, but in doing it.

— *Greg Anderson*

The first aspect of the **Wheel of Life** to consider is joy.

How do you define joy? Will more unstructured time make you more joyful?

In your Encore, you may not have the same markers of accomplishment that you did in your work life. Life in the workplace often operates at a cadence driven by customer needs, goal setting, and performance reviews. Raising a family has definite progress markers from pre-kindergarten to college graduation. In your Encore, there's a fresh opportunity to find or define new milestones to establish goals or celebrate accomplishments. These markers are important in providing tangible sources for satisfaction.

Some people believe joy comes from the combination of *service* and *engagement*. *Service* we define as remaining useful to society though offering your skills and wisdom both at home and in your community, whether as a volunteer or paid employee. *Engagement* is being connected to your community and circle of family and friends by showing up or initiating special events and fun activities. Or, as Woody Allen once cracked, "99% of life is showing up."

As you age, it can be tempting to start justifying skipping out on some activities or social functions, thus missing out on important connections to others. An example of this might be attending a sporting event in person vs. watching it on television. While it's true that traffic, parking costs, moving through crowds and navigating often inaccessible spaces can all present significant obstacles, it's also true that the energy of experiencing the pageantry, energy of the crowd and fellow fans, and being a part of something larger than yourself can provide benefits that extend past the event itself. Joy can be experienced as an individual event, but is often greatly enhanced when shared with others.

Some people never retire—they just move into a part-time work mode. Some people find their joy in continuing to contribute their hard-earned wisdom and intellectual capital. This could look like a volunteer role in local organizations, a position on an advisory board, consulting in your field, or even a part time job in a completely different field like substitute teaching or working at a nursery. If work brings you joy, there's no reason to stop working.

Hildy's Story

A hiker friend of mine knows of a couple getting ready to retire from their lucrative careers in the gas and oil industries. Instead of kicking back and vacationing on their well-earned retirement savings, this couple chose to join the Peace Corps. They're shipping out to a tropical island to teach business leadership to indigenous populations with fewer resources than Westernized nations, as well as teaching young women to play soccer.

There's no limit for you to remain useful to society. Regardless of culture, the human need for connection and purpose remains strong at any age. One of our favorite stories is the *Giving Tree* by Shel Silverstein. This children's story chronicles the relationship between a young boy and a tree. The tree gives the boy a place to play, his apples to sell and his trunk for a boat. In the end, all the tree has left is an old stump but he's happy when the boy, now an old man comes to sit on it. While the boy could've shown the tree more gratitude for the gifts the old tree offered him, the moral of story is being useful in your old age even with diminished capacity can be joyful. ✸

Ann's Story

My mother-in-law suffered from Alzheimer's disease. Even though she was impaired and couldn't do much in terms of being on her own any longer, when she was still able to visit our home, she took great pleasure in folding the laundry for my family. That way, she could still participate in household chores and was graciously recognized for her contributions. This is one example of a simple chore can contribute to being joyful about engaging in family routines and being of service to others. ✺

Create New Routines for Structure

When you retire, you may find a tremendous amount of time on your hands—but paradoxically, the days pass swiftly and before you know it, months have passed with not much to show for it. To avoid the *circumstantial depression* (not to be confused with *clinical depression*) that can plague retirees who lack purpose and/or structure, it can help to learn how to live in the moment and create daily rituals that are extremely fulfilling.

Think about what activities you want to start—or stop—doing, as well as what current activities you want to do more of—or less of—or to remain the same.

Joy Exercise

You can download Encore exercise from our website at https://yourencoreteam.com/. Consider doing the Joy exercise once a year at the beginning of the year or on your birthday to maximize your joy.

Ann's
Joy

Do More   Do Less

Journaling
Time in Nature
Cultural Adventures
Reading
Writing

Taking on work projects I don't
want to do
Over-packing my schedule
Worrying about money
and Social Security
going defunct

Start Doing

Meditate more
consistently
Read poetry with Steve

Start playing bridge
Having more fun

Feeling like i have to be
doing something every
minute to stay on top
of all aspects of my life

Operating at the
same pace and
intensity I did
20 years ago

Stop Doing

Doing yoga
Playing water polo
Eating as cleanly as
possible

Keep Doing

Ann's Sample Joy exercise

Hildy's Sample Joy exercise

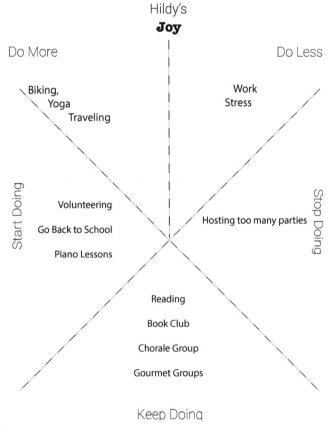

Hildy's
Joy

Do More   Do Less

Biking,
Yoga
Traveling

Work
Stress

Start Doing

Volunteering

Go Back to School

Piano Lessons

Hosting too many parties

Stop Doing

Reading

Book Club

Chorale Group

Gourmet Groups

Keep Doing

Hildy's Story

My paternal grandfather John was the master of ritual. Throughout my childhood, he came to live with our family on and off. Every morning, he took great pleasure in dressing in a three-piece suit. Every afternoon, he enjoyed a walk, donning a dapper hat for the activity. Every day, he ate nearly the exact same meal: one boiled egg, one piece of toast, and one cup of tea at breakfast. One slice of ham on white bread, and a piece of pound cake—cut into twelve perfect squares—for his daily lunch. He ate a piece of beef, potatoes, and a green vegetable for dinner, with rice pudding for dessert.

If he gained one pound on the scale in the morning, then Grandpop had no rice pudding that day. He kept copious notes in copybooks of racetrack conditions, weather, and winners of various horse races, constantly refining his system for betting on the horses. He was always busy; industrious, even. He was an avid reader and stayed abreast of world news to keep himself informed. ❀

As she moved into her 90s, my mother has come to appreciate some of Grandpop's daily habits. The ability to control your world becomes more important, much like the rituals we develop over time, which become a source of ongoing comfort in their routine. Some people may find joy in their Encore years in transforming the highly disciplined rhythms of their day from the traditional "9-to-5" structure to one that adapts that to the changes in their natural biorhythms. An example that takes this into account comes from a friend—formerly a small business owner with a very rigid schedule—who now luxuriates in the ability to sleep in and stay up late writing stories, a dormant passion that came back to life after retirement.

You too will be able to create new routines and activities to structure your day, to guard against becoming sedentary and isolated. The portrait of old age in American media is often painted as a dismal—disenfranchised and depressed adults, watching hours of television as the world swirls by them. But at the opposite end of the spectrum, consider this: there are older athletes still competing in Masters sports and living life to the fullest. In the book, *Goddesses Never Age*, noted women's health expert Dr. Christiane Northrup introduces the notion of "Happy, Healthy, Dead" as a worthy goal. She offers her mother as a prime example of someone who defied the stereotyping of aging by continuing to climb mountains, hike, and explore the world— well in her late 80s. Both Dr. Northrup and her mother prefer to engage joyfully with the world, remaining active as long as possible, rather than waiting for chronic illness or death to claim them.

Dr. Andrew Weil—an American physician, author, spokesperson, and advocate for holistic health and integrative medicine—talks about this as the "compression of morbidity," an approach which endeavors to reduce the risk of chronic illness through proactive, healthy habits. While you can't prevent the inevitability of aging, you can try to compress the dying period into as short a period as possible. Successful compression of morbidity means that you don't spend all your savings on long, drawn-out medical procedures, concerning and consuming the lives of your loved ones—instead, you're able to avoid some of the indignities of being a chronic patient. Ideally, you get to enjoy healthier productive years of your life. For those already dealing with a chronic illness, there's great value in designing and practicing the best health habits and supportive regimes possible to mitigate the impact of the chronic illness on both the quality of life and potential for compression of morbidity.

In a 1980 article from the *New England Journal of Medicine* called "Aging, Natural Death, and the Compression of Morbidity," author James Fries— a researcher on aging and death— writes that as humans, we "...don't wear out, we rust out," and that the first signs of morbidity or death start to occur around age 55. At the time of his study, the average age of death in America was 75, so for twenty years you can be in a state of increasing misery if you are dealing with chronic disease or increased health risks. He therefore advocated for disease and disability *prevention*— that you can remain vigorous and vital until shortly before death if you make conscious, powerful decisions around health.

Seniors who age gracefully tend to be very healthy and active on a consistent basis. For those with mobility issues or chronic illnesses, there are many fun options like aqua therapy, adaptive athletic endeavors (including skiing), and physical therapies that can stimulate body while soothing the mind and spirit. Wherever you are on the activity lifestyle spectrum, it's natural to want to remain relevant and visible in society. In the words of Doris Lessing as she entered menopause: "I don't want to be invisible."

What Will You Do with Your Bounty of Time?

Neuroscientists say your perception of time speeding up is due to the lack of experiencing new things—in short, our brain doesn't have to work as hard to process the familiar. Dr. Richard A. Friedman—a professor of clinical psychiatry and the director of the psychopharmacology clinic at the Weill Cornell Medical College, notes: "It's simple: if you want time to slow down, become a student again. Learn something that requires sustained effort; do something novel."

During your Encore, *joy* might mean *travel* for you. Foreign travel is at the top of many people's "bucket lists." The "travel bug" comes from the novelty of seeing sights you might never see or experience from your armchair. Traveling expands your thinking by providing great brain stimulation and new social experiences. If you're lucky enough to afford it, this could mean worldwide treks. Universities offer many travel options to explore the world, with diverse tours of historical venues with knowledgeable professors as your guide.

One example of educational travel is the Road Scholar program, whose mission is all about inspiring people through lifelong learning, discovery, and travel. This program offers learning adventures, where you can engage with expert instructors while building new friendships through shared experiences. Elder hostels are popping up all over the world just in time for aging Baby Boomers that need to travel on a budget. Hostels have always been popular for students who need to travel on a budget but as the largest demographic ages into retirement a new market has emerged. Elder hostels offer both local cultural tours in major metropolitan areas, like Chicago, San Francisco, Atlanta, or New York—as well as educational cruises and adventures, which include meals, lodging, and activities both throughout the US and internationally. Elder hostels are also a great boon for single people, as they don't charge as many other organizations do.

A slow crisscross of the country in a car or rented Airstream or minivan camping could be attractive, educational, affordable, and build new neural pathways. Many of the "hippies" of the 1960s are now entering their Encore years—the iconic VW bus that was so compelling during the Summer of Love was targeted for launch as an electric vehicle for this special demographic. You don't have to be uncomfortable camping any longer. The new trend for more affluent retirees is called "Glamping", short for **glamorous camping**. Beautiful tree houses, yurts, and tent cabins in exotic worldwide locations can be found on several glamping websites. You can have all the comforts of home—but in much more exotic locations!

Another economical travel option is to swap houses with another family somewhere else in the world. House swapping often includes the swapping of cars and the sharing of local discounts and club memberships. In this scenario, you post pictures of your home and amenities on a verified home exchange website and email with prospective families. Shelley Wise, an expert in the home exchange business, noted the popularity of house swapping as reflected by the surge in "over-70 clubs" to choose from. While there are plenty of opportunities here for joyful experiences, she advises careful research to ensure you're well educated in the process and potential pitfalls before engaging in a home exchange.

As always, you can check out the lists of top destination sites in the United States for shorter local trips. Retirees who want to see the sights of the United States often make checklists for their vacations like visiting every state, every US ballpark, every National Park, or every Presidential Library. There's an online list of 200 of America's greatest treasures, updated annually, called "Ultimate USA Wonders," which you can use to create your own travel "bucket list." Many universities even offer their own travel programs—which can be another way to travel and connect with new people with some common shared history.

Hildy's Story

A friend from my chorale group is a world traveler. Born in South America, she's lived all over the United States. She had plans for travel in her retirement, but her dear husband became very ill. She cared for him in her home for 10 years until his death. Now, she travels to visit family and friends all over the world and takes trips with her girlfriends—skiing, hiking and sightseeing—while she still can, even though she's well into her 70s. This wasn't the retirement she envisioned, by any means. She expected to take those trips with her husband. She says, "If you want to make God laugh—make plans." Even though she was housebound for over 10 years, she still wouldn't trade a day she spent with her husband for anything else in the world. Her travels now are still joyful, albeit differently—she's remained healthy and hearty, and she has one foot out the door when any opportunity to travel presents itself. ⊛

Of course, the most inexpensive way to keep time from speeding up is to embark on adventures through the pages of a good book. It's free with a library card and can stretch your mind in all kinds of directions. Consider joining or starting a book club to share your reactions to what you're learning and reading with others—all the while making new connections.

If travel isn't really your thing and you prefer to stay home, find joy in hobbies you never had time for while caring for a family, working full time, or doing both. Learn a new language, or take up a musical instrument. Take a class, or teach yourself how to crochet, create mosaics, or learn your way around a garden. Consider joining a card group, a bocce or bowling league, enroll in a poker tournament, or learn how to play billiards—there aren't any limitations on what's possible, so look for the one that best suits your personality and physical ability.

Exercising to remain healthy, vibrant, mobile, strong, and flexible is another important factor as you age, especially in terms of compressed morbidity. Exercise can be both joyful and a marvelous social outlet. As the Baby Boomers have aged, there's been a marked increase in hiking and bicycling, activities that are both conducive to ongoing health and promote social engagement. Hiking, walking, and yoga are especially popular among women as they age, with spas and resorts specifically targeting Boomer women with new programs that include yoga retreats or hiking vacations. There are swim vacations and chorale camps for adults. Pretty much any popular hobby has groups that you can meet up with to engage with others who share your passion. For people with chronic illness or mobility limitations, there are also many options to meet and join up with others to stay active and as healthy as possible.

On the craftier side of things, there are knitting and quilting circles in nearly every community of the United States and the world. Consider joining a Soul Collage group to get some guidance on creating vision boards. A Soul Collage is an inexpensive means of artistic expression—using pictures that you pull from magazines that are attractive to you, that speak to your "soul." You will typically have a theme for the type of collage, when engaging with a Soul Collage group, where participants will then cut and paste the images together, thus interpreting what these images communicate. Having experienced one of these workshops with Seena Frost, the founder of Soul Collage, we found it was a very interesting way to get in touch with our intuition and the experience created tools with deep personal meaning that have helped us with some of the challenges we've faced. Soul Collage groups meet and create cards around themes and share what they the cards are saying about their lives. In that spirit, we encourage readers to explore Pinterest, an online visual repository, a great option that caters to both the technologically savvy and those less familiar with navigating the worldwide web. You can search for specific images, recipes, or ideas or you can "pin" them to your different boards as you come across things in the online world you'd like to revisit or share.

Consider creating a vision board for what retirement joy could look like for you. It could be a poster board, a Pinterest board, or sketched mural. Gather images that are evocative of the retirement life you'd like to live—from images online or physical images taken from magazines or other media. Keep this **Life Stage** up somewhere you can see and revise it on a yearly basis if it helps inspire you to manifest joy in your life.

Simple Pleasures

What are your simple pleasures?

Joy doesn't have to be expensive or require a lot of effort like traveling the world. By being *present* and *observant* in your day-to-day life, you can practice gratitude and increase the number of simple things you do daily that brings you pleasure. What small things can you do to spark joy?

They don't have to be expensive. You can create your own list, of course, but to get you started, we've provided some food for thought below.

Ideas to Incorporate into Daily Routines

- Sing in the shower
- Send a quick group "I love you" text
- Have your favorite ice cream on a hot day
- Hide gratitude notes in the home of family or friends
- Buy fresh flowers every week
- Watch a sunset with your favorite music playlist
- Set the table in grand manner
- Nap on the beach
- Sleep in late
- Binge watch a series
- Catch up friends and family on social media
- Take a walk and explore the natural world

Set reminders on your phone or add joyful activities to your calendar to remind you to do what you love to do. Of course, you should also plan to indulge yourself with *your* guilty pleasures—whatever those might be. Your Encore might encompass all these simple pleasures or ideas for a joyful life—it's not an either/or situation.

Having a plan and a schedule of joyful activities may make your free time feel more structured, but you should also be careful not to overdo it— otherwise, you might be *working* at retirement instead of *enjoying* it! Balance, like beauty, is in the eyes of the beholder, meaning you has to be very aware of what their specific needs are and honor them vs. emulating what a friend or loved one does in their Encore. Remember Oscar Wilde's words of wisdom: "Everything in moderation, including moderation."

Ideally, having a long-term plan will keep you from becoming isolated. When you're facing loneliness, it's tough to keep a joyful outlook. Your social circle naturally tends to narrow as you age, and many friends move away or precede you in death. In your Encore, it'll take active participation on your part to keep up with old friends and continue to make new friends.

Bright Idea

As you age, your health or wealth may impose limits to your opportunities for travel. If you have mobility issues or a chronic disease, more careful planning is needed to prepare adequately for travel. Consider hitting your "bucket list" destinations in your 60s and 70s before any health infirmities make travel difficult for you or your traveling partner/s. You can travel locally more easily in your 80s where you speak the language and top medical help is nearby.

Most of the discussion on joy in this section is about proactively charting your course, which requires physical ability/mobility and—to some extent, financial solvency—for activities or lessons. One of the sayings on the yoga mat I used is, "Practice yoga so you can stay active as you age." Keep your joy goals in mind when you're working through the **Money** sections of this book.

 **Joy Reflection**

What brings you joy today?

_____

_____

_____

_____

_____

What's the most vibrant and exciting vision you can create for yourself for the rest of your life?

_____

_____

_____

_____

_____

What might you need to change to continue your joyful activities?

_____

_____

_____

_____

_____

How will you incorporate simple pleasures?

_____

_____

_____

_____

_____

_____

How can you still contribute to the greater good?

_____

_____

_____

_____

_____

_____

How can you remain visible and relevant in the word?

_____

_____

_____

_____

_____

_____

Chapter 6

Connections

A man once told Buddha, "I want happiness."

Buddha replied, "First. Remove 'I'—that's ego.

Then, remove 'want'—that's desire.

And now all you're left with is Happiness."

– Guatama Budda

Who Will Take Care of Me?

We know intuitively that remaining socially engaged is good for your mental health. Respected family therapist Virginia Satir believes we need four hugs a day for survival. We need eight hugs a day for maintenance. We need twelve hugs a day for growth. Lack of human connection is why solitary confinement is such an effective torture. Don't torture yourself in your Encore years! Whatever the right combination is to bring you joy, remaining connected will be a part of that journey.

A recent Japanese study set out to prove the need for connection, concluding that those with higher social connection have less stress. Reducing your stress can also help you reduce your risk for stress-inducing illnesses, like situational depression or high blood pressure. Consider how to remain connected with your family, friends and community to avoid the isolation that aging in your Encore can bring.

"Go-To" People

Who are your "Go-To" people today? Surprise! Those people may change throughout the course of your Encore years. You may have a social network at work that ends abruptly when you retire. If you've changed jobs you know this is true. Neighbors and friends move away—and so do children. You must be proactive in retirement in making connections and new friends or risk becoming isolated.

Challenge yourself to create and maintain relationships with people of all ages, and different personality types. It's so easy to fall prey to living in an "age ghetto," where all your connections are with people in your same age bracket. Seniors who are socially active and maintain connections with both younger and older friends report higher levels of happiness and remain healthier until the end.

Bright Idea

While engaging with your children and grandchildren is helpful, why not also consider places to volunteer or learn new things? You'll be interacting with a diverse group of people, especially those younger than you.

If you can play a musical instrument, or have the ability to teach poetry or some kind of visual or performing art, consider donating your time at elementary schools or after-school programs where the budgets for the arts may have been cut. Consider being a museum docent—you'll learn about the latest in art or history, while sharing your new-found knowledge with other art or history enthusiasts. You might also consider becoming a foster for abandoned or abused animals until they can be placed in a permanent homes—maybe even your own!

Ann's Story

When our eldest daughter attended a local co-op preschool, I kept hearing story after story about Nana. The teachers kept mentioning what day Nana would be at school for the first time to meet the three year-olds. Luckily, I was working my shift at the school when Nana walked

62

in and all the children went running up to her with hugs and kisses. Then she went over to the piano, picked a lucky child to help open the top of the keyboard, and then started playing "Hello, Dolly.". Transfixed, some of the children danced, others sang along, and some of them just smiled.

I learned later through "the mommy grapevine" that Nana lived in the local senior housing facility. Nana walked to the school on special days, had never been married, and deeply loved being "Nana" to the children. As a former teacher, she could share her passion for music, connect with children, and offer a non-judgmental, caring ear to many of the parents, who benefited from her years of experience. She was a true gift to our community—one of many ways that people find meaning in their Encore years. ❀

One exciting idea on benefits of cross-generational interaction is being tested with the co-location of preschools in nursing homes. A 2016 article in the *Atlantic* featured a Seattle school taking this approach and seeing great rewards for both the children and the seniors. Older adults can be very patient and kind with the young children, and young children aren't as frustrated by the slower speech or movement of older residents. Both preschoolers and assisted-living adults enjoy music programs together. Older adults often enjoy reading to the preschoolers or admiring their artwork and crafts. In one example, a 90 year-old with Alzheimer's become more mentally present when she entered a roomful of small children. The staff theorized the sound of children playing accessed some part of her brain that remembered her child-rearing years. The kids make the seniors laugh—and although the combination of assisted living and nursery school colocation isn't commonplace yet, there are a number of videos online sharing this approach, which viewers eagerly share with one another in the hopes that colocation will become a more common phenomenon, and a way for generations to benefit one another.

Who You Gonna Call?

No matter where you are on the wheel on current social connections, you should have a list of people to call in case you need:

- A ride or support in the emergency room
- A daily chat
- To share your new experiences
- To celebrate the holidays
- To make tough financial decisions
- Advice
- To work through a problem (or complain or rant!)
- An objective opinion

Statistically friends who've lived near each other for years often end up moving away from each other in their retirement. While this might secure their finances in their Encore years, some people may undervalue the connections they have to their existing community and friends. The dry cleaner who knows your first name, the coffee shop that knows what you mean when you say, "The usual," or the Chinese take-out place that recognizes your voice on the phone—these kinds of connections take years to cultivate, and anchor you in a community. The gourmet group, the cyclist group, the yoga studio, the local library branch, the knitter's "stitch-n-bitch", the book club, the beer or wine clubs you belong to in your mid-life—those connections could be harder than you think to replace in a new community. Old friends who knew you "way back when," and the family that'll stand by you no matter what—still more connections that can't be replaced easily.

However, if you do have move away—whether it's by choice or by financial necessity— you must proactively rebuild your social network. Volunteering in a new community is a great way to establish new connections. For people whose religion plays a central part of life, the natural first step in a new community is visiting the local place of worship for your faith. Consider hosting an open house in your community, to meet the new neighbors and introduce yourself. Online sites like Meet Up and Next Door are other quick ways to find out what's available and happening in your new town. You can also make an effort to remaining in touch via social media outlets like Instagram, Facebook, Google Hangouts and Facetime, Skype, or What's App instant messaging services to remain connected to your old network.

If you're lucky enough to live into your 80s or 90s, be prepared for some of your doctors and caregivers to retire—after all, it may be *their* Encore, too! You may need to strategically think through all the professionals and people you rely upon to stay healthy and connected. If you opt to move away, be prepared to start over building your network of social and professional connections. Consider asking others to share their trusted advisors with you and maybe ask for referrals in the area for professionals—from doctors and dentists to estate planners, you'll need to rebuild your connections from the ground up. Plan to interview new advisors and doctors to make sure they're a good fit for you. This is another good reason to remain socially active—you may have a lot of talking to do!

Network of Support

Who'll be in my network as I near the end of my life?

Think about all people in your network of support. The *professionals* are paid experts you rely on for advice, while your *daily living contacts* are people who help you with day-to-day activities. Listing all your *health support personnel*—including the numbers of local emergency rooms or urgent care, as well as your medical proxy or person who holds power-of-attorney—could help in a crisis. List important friends, family and neighbors who'd need to be notified when you die—both for memorial services and matters of estate, but also so beloved friends don't find out after it's too late to memorialize you with the other people who have been important in your life.

Fostering Connection

Consider all the people whom you've touched in some way over your life and all of those you've called friends—it's interesting to reflect on patterns of friendship in your life, what drew you to become friends, what sustained those friendships, and what caused some connections to end. Social scientists look very closely at the notion of *reciprocity* in relationships—essentially, your personal "talking/listening" ratio. When there's an imbalance in how much one person listens or talks, there can be a subtle shift in that friendship over time. Noticing this can invite new and more mindful interactions with current and future friends.

As you age, first your level of activity will likely drop off, followed by a drop in the number of people you interact with, the number of outings you take, the number of times you plan outings, your willingness to drive at night, and even the type of vacations you can take— eventually, even routine housework can become a challenge. This is especially true if your partner precedes you in death, and you aren't able to shoulder their contributions to the household, such as cooking, cleaning, or taking out the trash.

There are always alternative solutions to compensate for lack of skills (or inclination.) If you can afford it, consider hiring a companion to make your meals and drive you to do your errands—there are websites like Task Rabbit that specifically cater to people who need help with odd jobs at a modest cost. If finances are an issue or you're on a fixed income where every penny counts, reach out to local social services like Meals on Wheels, who deliver food daily to homebound adults who have trouble cooking for themselves. Contact local charities or community groups that offer driving services for older adults. Expand your own skills by tapping into vast internet resources of "How-To" videos on everything from plumbing to cooking.

Network of Support Exercise

You can download Encore exercise from our website at

https://yourencoreteam.com/. Use the Network of Support exercise to

ensure you have gathered names and numbers of important resources.

Professional	Health Support	Daily Living Support	End of Life Support
Lawyer	Primary Care Doctor	House Cleaner	Hopice Doctor
Tax Accountant	Eye Doctor	Gardener	Hospice Nurse
Financial Planner	Dentist	Hairdresser	Health Power of Attorney
Insurance Agent	Advise Nurse	Handyman	Estate Executor(s)
Banker	Local Hospital	Plumber	Will/Trust Attorney
Broker	Local Urgent Care	Transportation(taxi)	Spiritual Advisor
Trainer	Dermatologist	Alarm Company	
	Cardiogist	Groceries	
	GI Doctor	Meals On Wheels	
	Audiologist		
	Physical Therapist		
	Massage Therapist		
	Mental Therapist		
	Other Specialties		

Personal				
Family	Close Friends	Close Neighbor	Church/Spiritual Network	Social Network

Ann's Story

After my mother died, I watched my father transform from the witty raconteur of his local watering hole to "Lord of His Living Room," holding court with family members kind enough to bring the world to him. Although both his children and grandchildren offered numerous opportunities for him to engage in a widowers' support group, to take lunch at a local senior center, or to take him on outings to get him out of the house, he insisted on setting his own pace and choosing his own activities. While we constantly worried about his health and hermetic existence—and continued to offer ideas and companionship—he reveled in living as a misanthrope who only interacted with others when he needed something. While we didn't want this for ourselves and felt very ashamed when other relatives or neighbors asked after him—he was *adamant* that he was living his life the way he wanted, without the interference of others. We've learned that each person is the architect of their own life at every age. Our offers of help were perceived as intrusive and unwanted, so we had to be peaceful with a decidedly *un*-peaceful situation.

As fate would have it, one day he fell out of his chair— luckily, our nephew was there setting up a new television set, rushed downstairs to help him, and was aghast when he saw his frail, almost 86-year-old grandfather laying on the floor. It took an "intervention" by a neighbor to get our father's permission to call 911, where he was admitted to the hospital and then released to a skilled nursing facility to regain his strength. I flew out to be with him, and chuckled as he held court now with us scattered around his bed, watching him drink one of his favorite chocolate milkshakes we'd brought him. The next day as I headed over to support making plans for his future, we got a call that he was found unresponsive in his bed, so my youngest sister and I rushed to the facility to witness him being loaded on gurney into an ambulance. We talked our way into riding with him, and he roused a bit so we could tell him we loved him and were there for him before he became unresponsive again. In the ER, a flurry of activity greeted us, and despite knowing he was a **DNR** *(Do Not Resuscitate)*, a Respiratory Therapist already had started a breathing treatment which was agitating our father, so I called out, "Stop!" and pulled the doctor away to better understand his prognosis.

When he indicated he had one to two days left, I told him he wouldn't want this given his DNR status, so the doctor agreed to let his remain in the ER for a few hours for observation and removed the oxygen. When he started getting agitated again, we called the nurse to see and she asked the physician if she could give him something for the pain. As the morphine kicked in, we told him we loved him, lowered the lights, and played some of his favorite music so he could die peacefully with his "bookend" daughters holding each of his hands, sailing away to Dave Brubeck's "Take Five."

My five siblings and I went through a lot together growing up, so after creating a beautiful memorial service for him at the church were he and my mother were married serenaded by bagpipes and laid to rest with beautiful flowers with my mother's ashes, we did a special ritual together. We got a limo, and took a shared trip down memory lane to our old houses, schools, and hang out places to celebrate the end of an era and the start of a new one. ✸

Guarding Against Elder Abuse

The dark side of being older and dependent is the prevalence of elder abuse, which commonly presents in any combination of three ways: *mental, physical* and *financial*. Caretakers can become overwhelmed with caring for an older relative, frustrated at the time and effort it consumes. Treating an elderly person like a child, talking down to them, shouting at them, isolating them from friends or loved ones, or causing them emotional anguish (elders suffering from Alzheimer's are especially vulnerable to this type of abuse) are all examples of *elder mental abuse. Physical elder abuse* might take the form of withholding food or drink, shoving, hitting, or pinching an elderly person out of frustration, or physical caretaking neglect (bedsores, infections, withholding medications). Finally, some unscrupulous people try to take advantage of the elderly though financial elder abuse, which can include—but are by no means limited to—scams, Pyramid schemes, internet "phishing," credit card fraud, or seizing assets or property (via power of attorney or outright theft). Elderly people in assisted care facilities are often extremely vulnerable to this type of abuse. Any combination of these behaviors may be classified as abuse against the elderly.

Hildy's Story

The elderly mother of a friend was living in a continuous cycle of both physical and financial abuse at the hands of her drug-addicted adult son. He locked away the food and refrigerator, and wouldn't let her eat unless she wrote him exorbitant checks. She "fell" often, once breaking her wrist while in his "care." Finally, my friend was able to remove her mother from the abusive home, but it took a lot of effort, a "paper trail" of evidence and a court order to get the abusive family member evicted from their mother's house. My friend needed to sell that home to provide for her mother's long-term care. Before the abusive family member vacated the property, he wreaked havoc by destroying many of the valuable items and necessitating repairs to the house itself, jeopardizing the income from the sale of assets that his mother was dependent upon for her financial survival. The upshot of this story is this: we never want to believe that a family member would be capable of taking advantage of other family members in this way—but because people can be unpredictable, it's always good to have a legal "safeguard" in place before you ever need it, so that should the worst happen, you have options and recourse available. ✺

What About Love?

Connection can be about finding a new love at any age. As you age, your ideas about romance are likely to change. Modern research on aging and romance indicates a significant difference between young love and mature love. According to a recent *Psychology Today* article on love and aging, the Top-5 most highly rated elements of successful romantic relationships for the older adults were honesty, communication, companionship, respect, and positive attitude, whereas as the Top-5 most highly rated elements of romantic relationship success for younger adults were love, communication, trust, attraction and compatibility. With age, individuals seem to choose a partner with whom they can share their diverse life experiences in an open and positive way, while younger people seem to select partners with whom they can create experiences based on shared emotions.

You may have heard the saying "Women grieve, and men replace." The Pew Research Center's statistics bear this adage out, reporting, "…previously married men are more likely than previously married women to have remarried [64% vs. 52%]." It's also encouraging to note that this statistic also indicates that 40% of older adults who remarry do so because they feel that sharing a life together with another person brings comfort and security—whatever life brings your way, consider whether part of it includes a good partner with whom you can share your Encore journey.

There's an old saying— "Just because there's snow on the roof, doesn't mean the fire is out in the basement." Often, people from younger generations assume that sex is part of life that falls wayside as we age—this couldn't be further from the truth. According to the 2009 *Community Health Nursing* book, sex between residents in nursing homes is commonplace—so common, in fact, that there's been an uptick in reports of sexually transmitted diseases (STDs) in nursing homes over the recent years, due to a lack of safe sex education and practices with older adults. As long as you're protecting your health (and heart)—why *shouldn't* a happy, healthy sex life be included as part of living your best Encore life? Human connections thrive with love, affection, and the physical comfort of being touch and held, and sexual activity is a natural offshoot of that connection. And while your childbearing years may be well-behind you, if you're engaging in sexual activity with a new partner, it's important to make your physician aware of it, to ensure that your health is protected and you're educated on how to prevent contracting an avoidable (and uncomfortable) STD. Baby Boomers who grew up in the age of the Pill may be uncomfortable or unaccustomed to using condoms, so it is important to have them handy to prevent chlamydia, syphilis, gonorrhea, and AIDS.

Mature marriage, or remarriages later in life come with their own set of concerns. You might have to consider your own health and financial support systems before you consider marrying during your Encore years. Before formally joining your lives together, consider:

- Will you be capable (physically, emotionally, financially) to shoulder the care that might be required?
- What would the impact be to your heirs—financially, emotionally, and legally?
- What do you do with your Will and Trusts?
- Will you inherit your new partner's debt if you marry?
- Who will be the person making decisions on your behalf, financially, medically, legally, and in terms of end-of-life care?
- Is your partner's family supportive of your relationship?

Some people want to marry or remarry in their Encore years for religious or moral reasons, while others opt to marry for financial or end-of-life care decisions. Remember that there are legal alternatives to marriage, which will allow your partner to remain with you in hospitals or grant them the legal right to make end-of-life care decisions on your behalf. There are even legal documents, which can be drawn up to ensure that your partner will be cared for financially without marriage. If you're open-minded and proactive, there are a number of ways to ensure that an *Encore* partnership benefits both partners—and their families—whether or not you decide to walk down the aisle.

Hildy's Story

A colleague of my father's lost his wife when he was in his 70s. Within a year of becoming a widower, he'd started dating a vibrant woman in her 50s, who confided to my mother that she was reluctant to marry because she was afraid of eventually becoming his caregiver. Love won out, and they married, enjoying many happy years together, before the new wife was diagnosed with cancer. The widower—now a man in his 80s— cared for his second wife throughout her cancer treatments until her death. While on the surface, this story may not sound like a happy ending—it goes to show you that life is unpredictable, youth is no guarantee of longevity, and that a loving marriage—no matter your age—is worth its weight in gold, no matter how many years you're blessed to spend together. ✸

Connection Reflection

What do you look for in a good friend?

_____

_____

_____

_____

_____

_____

What's your process for making new connections?

_____

_____

_____

_____

_____

_____

If making connections is hard for you, what small steps can you take to get there?

_____

_____

_____

_____

_____

_____

And now all you're left with is Happiness."

What's your talking/listening ratio? What can you do to improve it?

Are you open to new romance or connection in your Encore?

Chapter 7

Environment

He who is in harmony with Nature hits the mark without effort
and apprehends the truth without thinking.

— Confucius

Your physical environment has a huge impact on your happiness in your Encore years. In planning for this stage of your life, you have many options to consider. At some point, there's strong possibility that you won't be able to live as independently as you did once, due to diminished capacity, health, or financial resource issues. As you age, you must consider the transition of your living arrangement options.

When Should You Make a Move?

Ideally, by age 75, you're already in the community and location where you plan to spend the rest of your days. Physical and cognitive changes will make it more difficult for you to pick up and move to a new community without significant effort—and likely, more than a little anxiety—for you and your loved ones. While it may be stressful and scary to think about leaving your home due as you age, it's better to start the conversation sooner rather than later to prevent feeling like you're overburdening your family. The last thing anyone wants is to have limited options and have to make split-second decisions of this magnitude, prompted by a crisis or medical emergency.

Once an elderly person has been admitted to the hospital, they aren't generally released from care back into their home without an official assurance that their home is still a safe place for them to be. This can therefore act as a "forcing function" which requires looking for an alternative living situation at a skilled nursing facility until the older person is well enough to return home with the proper modifications to their environment (e.g., area rugs removed to avoid fall risks, grab bars in the bathrooms, regular meal delivery, etc.). If home modifications to ensure ongoing safety aren't a possibility, it might be time to secure an alternative place to live. In this situation, options may prove limited by long waiting lists or the need to sell a home to pay for the new living environment or ongoing care.

Advantage and Disadvantages of Downsizing

You can benefit from downsizing your home and/or possessions while you're still alive. Downsizing gives you the opportunity to gift some of your belongings to the next generation, who often welcome family heirlooms like furniture, housewares, or irreplaceable items like family photos. For most people, there's nothing sadder than visiting an estate sale where buyers pick through an older person's treasures. Grieving family members don't always know what's valuable, what should stay in the family, or the backstory behind the items a person accumulates throughout their lifetime. The personal stories of how an heirloom came into the family can often only be told by the person who collected it, and unfortunately, many of these invaluable stories die when they do.

Additionally, selling off certain antiques or jewelry may provide necessary financial capital to fund your "bucket list" ideas, shared with younger generations to "plant seeds" for their future, or may be given to a charity of your choice.

Consider taking a picture of your most treasured items, and committing the story of why they're special to paper, before giving them away. Spend some time organizing and digitizing old photos with caption, dates, and places. Having an account of your travels and looking back at old photos is like walking down a memory lane, one that you can enjoy in a smaller space and easily take with you. These can also be a legacy treasure that you family would enjoy—after all, they may want to share your stories with future generations, as a means of keeping your memory alive. You don't have to be famous to create an autobiography that recounts your life, complete with pictures of your journey. Some people even discover a latent love of writing in compiling their memoir, recounting significant life events and adding a robust dimension to the family's history.

Hildy's Story

A business colleague told me she always wanted to live in a beach house, but as she and her husband neared retirement she realized that their financial constraints were such that this could never be a real option. However, she had a long-term, close friendship with three other couples, and they collectively decided to buy retirement homes in different desirable locations, each with 4 bedrooms. Their plan was to spend time with each other in the 4 different locations through the years, with each couple hosting a turn. My friend stayed in their hometown. While her location wasn't a "vacation" destination like the beach, the mountains or wine country, it had the added benefit that the circle of old friends could reconnect with the community they'd left behind when they moved away in retirement. Talk about community! ✿

Aging in a Senior Living Community

Many 55+ residential communities allow people to move from a single-family residence into a more modest home, often where some level of services are provided to residents. Some of these communities provide graduated care options so you can easily transition from a house to a condo or apartment or into a nursing home as your needs and ability evolve over time. These types of retirement communities often offer a variety of activities, food options, and other kinds of social entertainment to keep their aging community engaged with one another. In addition to outside grounds maintenance, some of these communities also have community pools, tennis courts, golf ranges, and dining halls for members who are unable to cook (or who prefer to have their meals taken care of for them.) Many also offer social connection activities like book clubs, bingo, concerts and day outings to movies and museums. Senior communities can be empowering for many, with a built-in social group you can tap into if you're so inclined. These communities generally range in price from modest to high-end.

Aging in Private Boarding Home

Caregivers offer rooms in private homes for older adults who need 24-hour supervision but aren't otherwise medically incapacitated. For patients with dementia or Alzheimer's who need monitoring or supervision, but don't require medical nursing supervision, this is often a good solution. These kinds of private homes typically offer a smaller, more intimate, "homey" environment, as compared to larger facilities where care might be more clinically focused. Private boarding homes are often located in tucked-away alcoves right in your own neighborhood, making it easy for you to enjoy visitors while still patronizing your local vendors like hairdressers, dentists, and doctors—while keeping your family secure in your ongoing care and safety.

Aging in Nursing Homes

Nursing homes provide full-time medical supervision for elderly patients who require more care than a home-care environment can provide. Some care facilities offer lifetime care for patients who turn over their assets and assign their Social Security and Medicare benefits to the organization. Though this may sound intimidating, this can be a good option if you need ongoing medical care or have limited financial resources. Many people find this kind of living situation to be the perfect option for both themselves and their families. Often, nursing homes are lovingly called "Stairways to Heaven," and the residents often refer to the staff as "Angels."

However, as previously noted in the section on elder abuse, these types of facilities can have a certain amount of risk, especially when a resident signs over their medical power of attorney rights and financial assets—so due diligence is a necessity as you consider this option. Finding the right fit for you or your loved one takes rigor, research, and clarification of priorities. It can help to take a step back and consider factors such as the current health status and projected health outlook of the prospective resident (e.g., medication management, incontinence care, mobility requirements, Alzheimer's/dementia care, need for onsite clinical staff, etc.) as well as their personal needs (meals, transportation, housekeeping, laundry) and social needs (activities, outings, support for hobbies, etc.) The more clear and honest you are with assessing the unique needs of the person, the more likely you'll be to have success exploring potential homes and eventually decide on the right facility. In addition to online searches, there are numerous place-ment counselors and specialized agencies that are experts at finding the right fit at the right time for the person in need of ongoing care.

In the Netherlands, an innovative nursing home offers students free housing in exchange for assisting seniors in learning new technology, sorting bills, performing daily tasks or errands, connecting with them over a cup of tea, and other meaningful ways of being of service to the elder generation. Like the colocation concept of preschools with nursing homes, this model of colocation has also proven to be a win-win for both the seniors and students, as each genera-tion benefits from being a part of their respective life experiences. This colocation model has also driven down the operational costs of the nursing home. Personally, we love the innovation of colocation in nursing home facilities to create more positive experiments with cross-genera-tional pollination in nursing homes, and hope that in coming years, Americans will embrace the possibility of this model as well.

Aging in Place

Staying in your own home can give active seniors a sense of control and empowerment, but as with most factors in your Encore years, there are also some important trade-offs you may not have considered:

- Will you be able to afford to pay for any help in the maintenance of your home, such as yard work, gardening, cleaning the gutters, or repairs?

- Will you be able to pay for any personal care or assistance required to stay in your home?

- Will you become isolated, if your ability to drive becomes compromised?

- Will your nutrition suffer, if you become unable to cook?

- Have you put off maintenance in your home, or will staying in your home require modifications?

- Will you have a family member or legal proxy available, should you become unable to make medical or legal decisions for yourself?

Consider getting your affairs in order if you want to "age in place" at home in your 60s and early 70s, and if you can afford to do so, "feather your nest" while you're able. Consider making some upgrades to your property: a new roof, solar energy options, tankless water heaters, new bathroom or kitchen fixtures, upgraded appliances, or home security options. There's a whole world of new technology available to assist you with staying in your home. Intel and GE have created some great home health solutions for monitoring movement in the home, your walking gait, the number of times the refrigerator opens, electronic tracking of your pill consumption, and a host of techniques for calling for help. Most health organization have mail-order prescription services and you can now Skype with a doctor for regular check-up or call an advice nurse with quick questions. Likewise, online vendors like Amazon and Instacart can now ship just about everything to your home—including, but not limited to—groceries, which can often be the greatest obstacle for seniors who can no longer drive but are otherwise independent.

Another consideration to aging in place is the problem of social isolation, if at some point you're no longer mobile. Online social connection is one great option, with many older adults now turning to social media to stay connected with friends and family. Pew Internet research statistics show that today, seniors and Baby Boomers aged 55 to 64 are the fastest-growing adopters of social media. Many Boomers want to age in place, especially after their own experiences caring for their aging parents.

If you do opt to remain in your home and you're alone, you should consider investing in a system like Lifeguard, that provides 24-hour monitoring and can call for help with just the press of the button on a pendant you can wear around the house and even in the shower.

Marketplace Power for Aging in Place

As the Boomers age and reach the tipping point of retirement, many marketing companies have begun to understand their evolving needs, and have started to cater to the older adult demographic. In the same way that parking spaces and public building provide for wheelchairs and handicapped access, a whole host of new products is emerging to make it easier for seniors to stay in their own homes. Even the product you buy will start to be packaged with the older adult in mind.

Communal Living

Though less common in the US than they are worldwide, multigenerational family homes are another option for you and your family to consider. In the 2010 US Census, 15% of Americans over the age of 65 reported living with non-spouse relatives. The combined concepts of aging in place and multiple generations of a family living together are appealing to many. Younger generations have the wisdom and history of the aging grandparents available, as well as the added benefit of childcare and the sharing of household chores and expenses. The elder generation may feel more valued, invigorated, and engaged with both their family and life in general. In this spirit, an architect at UC Berkeley has started designing small portable homes that can be placed on a small plot of land—often without any additional zoning required—for seniors to live close by, but with more privacy and independence. These tiny homes are called "Granny Pods" and they're on the market today.

Bright Idea

Learn and incorporate any **American Disabilities Act (ADA)** current requirements when designing any remodel, and create a cost-effective plan to execute these changes before you retire and/or need the changes. Why not enjoy a more sound and beautiful environment instead of waiting and remodeling for someone else's benefit?

Hildy's Story

Friends of mine chose to move into the husband's parents' home when his father passed away and it was evident that his mother couldn't live alone any longer. His mother didn't want to leave her home. This couple were empty nesters, and so they decided to sell their home. They invested their home sale proceeds in a retirement fund and moved in with the widow to care for her at home. This was a win-win family solution.

In my family, we opted for moving my mom in to our home at age 90. She lived alone for over 14 years in a large two story 5-bedroom home after my father passed away. She was reluctant to give up her independence, and friends had warned her to stay in her own home as long as she could. Ultimately, at 90 years of age, the stairs and her weak knee came to be too much. My brother and I helped Mom sell her home. She invested in remodeling one of the bedrooms in our home to add a bathroom suite, skylights and a garden window. It's a beautiful room and ADA compliant, in case she needs it in the future. She's enjoying the multi-age mash-up at our home between our friends and her grandkids. As one of her executors, it was a blessing to go through her possessions with her. She could tell me what possessions should stay in the family and what should go to charity! ✺

Bright Idea

If you're proactive, there are opportunities available for participating in a residential care home businesses where your meals, housework, and laundry are taken care of in a communal living arrangement—kind of like a home daycare facility, but for seniors who live in a home with a family. The monthly fees paid by elderly tenants can often help young couples afford a mortgage, while benefiting all parties through social connection, camaraderie, and a "chosen family" feeling.

Environment Exercise

You can download Encore exercise from our website at https://yourencoreteam.com/.   As you prepare to downsize your home or streamline your current living space this guide can help you as you sort through your belongings.

Environment Reflection

How do you take care of your home environment today? (Household, work, community, and/or world)?

_____

_____

_____

_____

_____

_____

How would you describe the shape and space that you occupy in the world?

_____

_____

_____

_____

_____

_____

If an anthropologist were to visit your home, car, place of work, what story would they tell about you?

_____

_____

_____

_____

_____

What resources do you hold most precious, and why?

_____

_____

_____

_____

_____

When you need to learn about how to do something, how do you go about it?

_____

_____

_____

_____

_____

If you want to age in place: Would you move to a home with no stairs?

_____

_____

_____

_____

_____

How could you make your current home accessible or ADA compliant?

_____

_____

_____

_____

_____

Chapter 8

Money

Retirement at 65 is ridiculous. When I was sixty-five I still had pimples.

– George Burns

Will I Have Enough?

George Burns may have been prophetic—saving for retirement isn't as easy to do as it was for the generations who preceded them. Reports from the Insured Retirement Institute indicate that Boomers haven't saved enough, and an even more recent study confirmed that of those Boomers who have been able to save money for retirement, the largest percentage of the demographic has saved $50k or less—even more concerning, fully 40% of Boomers haven't been able to save any significant amount for their retirement. Of the 60% who have been able to create savings, only 27% of Boomers surveyed felt confident that they've saved enough. The reality is harsh, and can be demoralizing: most Boomers won't have the same kind of retirement experience that their parents enjoyed, one where they're financially able to stop working and enjoy years of pure leisure time.

The Social Security Administration continues to increase the eligible age of full retirement, which is defined as, "... the age at which a person may first become entitled to full or unreduced retirement benefits." While you can start receiving benefits as early as age 62 or as late as age 70, there's a sliding scale based upon the year you were born available on the official Social Security Administration website and is excerpted below. The tail end of the Baby Boomer generation can't retire will full benefits until age 67. Generation X has already been pushed back to 70 years old to get Medicare and Social Security benefits. When surveyed, Americans say they plan to just keep on working at least in a part time capacity. Over a third of Baby Boomers plan to work until they're 70—health willing.

Financial planners recommend saving enough to replace 75% - 80% of your pre-retirement living costs. A wide variety of options exist for retaining as much of your retirement capital as possible. These include the Principal Principle (keeping the principal intact and living off the interest), the *Interest-Only Principle* (where you need to consider your average yield of your portfolio to derive your cash flow requirements), and *Fixed Deferred Annuities* (an interest-bearing account like a certificate of deposit that can provide a predictable interest rate while protecting your principal). This assumes you will leave the entire retirement savings to your heirs and you don't deplete your capital. Based on your unique circumstances, however, it's possible that you might not need to save as much money as the experts recommend.

Retirement Budget

Your yearly cost of living in retirement is needed to use the online retirement calculators. It can also help you budget today to save more for retirement. Multiple retirement calculators can help you figure out how much you will need to save. Most investment brokers and banks have online calculators, and some of our favorite calculators come from AARP and the Financial Mentor websites. Northwestern Mutual, a highly respected insurance and financial advisory firm, looks not only at assets saved for retirement but also at the key risks of retirement. They identify the following risks, and recommend putting in place a risk mitigation plan to deal with these potential risks:

Date of Retirement: Their metrics indicate 50% of people end up retiring four years earlier than they'd planned, due to changes in employment, illness, or unexpected family issues. Obviously, this affects not only the amount of money saved, but also adds a substantial period when you are going to be drawing from their retirement funds.

Longevity: How do you make sure your money lasts as long as you do? Sigmund Freud once said that "the organism wishes to die only in its own fashion," noting that he wanted to choose when he would die. As fate would have it, he did indeed achieve his goal, as his private physician, Dr. Max Schnur, administered morphine upon Freud's request when he was ready to end his life. Given that most of us won't follow suit, refer to our resources to help calculate your longevity and help you plan accordingly.

Long-Term Care: It's critical to ensure the costs of care for an unexpected event like a long-term illness is part of your financial planning if it isn't covered by your insurance or Medicare. Typically, the longer you wait to purchase long-term care, the more expensive it is.

Health Care Costs: US health care costs continue to rise despite legislative and other attempts to control costs to the consumers. Many people mistakenly think Medicare is "free," but there are many nuances and non-covered services to consider such as dental, vision, and orthotics. As prescription drug prices also continue to rise, supplemental insurance may be needed for those with acute or chronic conditions requiring daily medication.

Leaving a Legacy: For some, it may be very important to leave a financial legacy for loved ones, or a favorite philanthropic organization. This may require additional financial and tax planning given the lack of precise predictability of knowing how long you will live.

Market Trends, Inflation & Taxes: Careful thought needs to be given to long-term economic trends (both nationally and globally) that affect US inflation, tax rates, and economic stability. At a minimum, financial planning experts recommend building in a 3% inflation rate and reserving 10% for taxes.

Litigation Risk: While it may seem a dim possibility, it can be helpful to look at the risk of an adverse event at your home triggering a litigious chain of events such as a houseguest falling and injuring him or herself. Consider a robust umbrella policy to protect yourself so you can sleep better at night.

Remember, the amount of discretionary funds you've saved might alter the scale of the things on your "bucket list", but not the joy you'll derive from them. Money isn't everything. Revisit our section on Joy for more discussion on how to make the most of your golden years no matter your budget.

Budget Exercise

You can download Encore exercise from our website at https://yourencoreteam.com/. Create your own version of this template to help you think through what you will need for monthly run rate in retirement.

Case Study

We recommend that you walk through some basic math on your retirement estimates and budgeting. Below, we've provided a case study as an example.

Subject: Widow

Assets: Two pensions, widow's late husband's social security, two cars, two homes.

Case Study Specifics: Since subject is over 70, her IRA has a minimum distribution she is required to take out, or $12,000. Though able to take more, this amount is approximately the 4% recommended to ensure principle is not reduced.

Fixed Income Detail

Income	Name	Monthly Amount	Pay Day	Yearly Amount
	Pension 1	$930.30	2nd	$11,163.60
	Pension 2	$267.12	2nd	$3,205.44
	IRA Distribution	$1,000.00	5th	$12,000.00
	Social Security	$1,874.30	4th weds	$22,491.60
Total		$4,071.72		$48,860.64

Expenses

Fixed Expense			Due Day	Yearly Amount
Monthly	Cell Phone	$127.58	2nd	$1,530.96
	Electric Power & Gas	$150.00	3rd	$1,800.00
	Health Insurance	$194.25	5th	$2,331.00
	Mortgage	$985.87	6th	$11,830.44
	Cable	$33.00	15th	$396.00
	Internet	$153.92	22nd	$1,847.04
Yearly	Real Estate Taxes			$2,041.00
	Estimated Qtrly Taxes Fed		15th $621 / 4 qtrs	$2,484.00
	Estimated Qtrly Taxes State		15th $407 / 4 qtrs	$1,628.00
	insurance – Property 1		5th - $70.03 for 6 months	$343.06
	Insurance – Property 2		5th - $140.06 for 6 months	$798.38
	Allstate (2 cars)		5th - $180.33 for 6 months	$1,061.08
	Magazine Subscriptions		July	$24.00
	Medical Prescriptions		Jan, Apr, June, Sept	$50.00
	AAA Membership		Nov	$90.00
Total		$2,350.41		$28,204.96

Variable Expenses (Budget Planning)

Variable Expenses			Due	Yearly Amount
Desired Budget		$1,721.31		$20,655.68
Daily Living				
	Food	$500		
	Clothes	$300		$3600
	Drug Store	$200		
	Hair Appointments	$150		
	Dry Cleaners	$50		
	House Cleaner	$125		
	Shipping & Postage	$25		
Total		$1350.00		
Discretionary				
	Wine clubs	$50		$600
	Gifts & Cards	$240		$2400
	Dining Out	$200		
	Classes	$50		$600
	House Décor	$50		$600
	Handyman - plumber	$50		$600
	Gardener	$400		
Estimated		$1040.00		
Current Run Rate	Daily Living Estimate + Discretionary Estimate	$2390.00		
Budget Estimate	Target - Estimate	- $668.00		

Monthly Run Rate Budgeting

The goal of this exercise is to help you create a realistic budget so you're not depleting your investment capital too quickly. Your ideal budget should be: **Monthly Income - Average Monthly (Fixed + Variable Expenses)** The Case Study cited above details the projected expenses for a widow with a fixed income. If the subject doesn't adjust her budget to reflect her new financial constraints, each month she will be over budget by $668. The disconnect in the new budget originates in basic house maintenance which was previously performed by the subject's husband, labor for which she must now contract. The subject has several options: She might opt to sell one of the secondary cars or properties. The subject might also downsize into a smaller home, to bolster her fixed income. The subject might also adjust the amount she spends on discretionary spending—such as gifts and cards, wine clubs and dining out—to bring her back under budget, so her investment capital is not depleted.

We recommend that you go through more detailed **Money – Retirement Budget Estimate** exercises located in the digital resources to determine what your money needs will be, going to be in retirement. Use this template as guide to estimate fixed and variable costs in retirement.

Don't Hide the Treasure Map!

Leave clear details on where all your money is stashed (bank accounts, bonds, stocks, savings, etc.) and also what assets you own (home, automobiles, property, etc.) Most wills and trusts won't include details like account numbers, passwords, or mortgage and credit card information. Don't forget to list things like magazine, online subscriptions, and/or gym memberships, or other memberships that are on automated payments or that will continue to be billed after you die. Making sure that it's in a place that's both secure and accessible, make sure you've listed your login information and passwords to your social media accounts.

This kind of information can be organized on a digital worksheet, which should be updated no less than annually. Having clear direction on where to find your will and your important information inventory avoids the tedious work for your beneficiaries to settle your financial affairs.

Bright Idea

The Important Information Inventory Exercise serves a dual purpose. You can use it for planning your retirement and it additionally acts as the Rosetta stone for your survivors. Updating the inventory yearly and storing it with your trust/will is important to do on a regular basis. Update your inventory based on an annual trigger—like a birthday, anniversary, or even the 4th of July—to safeguard against the potential hassle of making your loved ones hunt for key information later.

Leave a note for your executor of your trust or will, instructing them to order 20 extra copies of your death certificate. Most financial organizations will require a copy of the death certificate to make changes to the accounts and transfer assets. You might also consider adding your executor to a joint account that can be used to pay for funeral, burial or financial fees for a tax attorney and/or your lawyer to execute the terms of the trust or will. The price of all stock and bond assets on the date of your death must be researched and reported for estate tax filings.

If you're resistant to documenting your assets and calculating your potential retirement needs, consider why it is that you find yourself resistant. For some of us, this resistance is rooted in the fear of dying, or in feeling the vulnerability of our mortality. For others, the deeply ingrained cultural or social taboos about talking about money matters create an emotional hurdle that many find difficult to leap. But you know the saying, "There are no pockets in shrouds," so consider letting your executor know your financial situation, and where your assets are located ahead of your death.

Important Information Inventory Exercise

You can download Encore exercise from our website at
https://yourencoreteam.com/. If you want to create your
own important document inventory content download the excel
version. This document should be shared with the executor of your estate and kept with your
will or estate documents.

Account Type	Account #	Phone #	Website	User Login	Password
Bank (s)					
Checking (s)					
Saving (s)					
Money Market (s)					
Certificates of Deposit (s)					
Debit Card (s)					
Bank (s)					
Retirement Plan 401K IRAs Roth IRAs SEPs SARSEP					
Broker Acct (s)					
Pension (s)					
Credit Card (s)					
Mortgage Lender					
Loans					

Insurance for Your Long-Term Care

Many people are vehement in not wanting to be a burden on their children or loved ones as they age. If moving in with family isn't an option for you, maybe it's time for you to consider a Long-Term Care insurance policy to cover the costs of medical equipment and in-home care, if you wish to age in place in your own home. If you require nursing home care, these types of policies will also cover some additional nursing home costs that Medicare may not cover. To find the best long-term insurance carriers, we suggest you consult Consumer Affairs who rates all the carriers and their benefits

Given the fact that many women take time away from the working world to care for children, aging parents, and other relatives, it's definitely a concern senior women often face the double challenge of having less saved with an average life span which has increased from 77 to 83. The key to peace of mind for both women and men is financial literacy and understanding the trade-offs for all key monetary decisions.

Ann's Story

A former client talked frequently about how miserable she was in her job, but felt she needed to continue working, worried as she was about not having enough money to retire. As a single woman with a great income, she'd saved a tremendous amount of money, stood to inherit a substantial sum from her father, and had a brother who was a multi-millionaire who'd promised to take care of her no matter what. Still, she worried every day about what would happen to her, and even remained at work while battling breast cancer and then Stage 4 ovarian cancers.

The time she spent worrying about money might have been better invested in focusing on her health and happiness. As a wise family friend said who'd started a home-based business after her husband became disabled and there wasn't enough money to support the family of 6 children, "Worry is like a rocking chair—it keeps you moving, but gets you nowhere." ⊛

Who Will Inherit My Treasures?

Do you have a will or an estate plan in place? If not, you've plenty of company. The American Bar Association's research reflects that every year, 55% of Americans die without a will or any kind of estate planning. *Wills* are a relatively simple legal document, stipulating how you want your property to be distributed and can also include your wishes for how any children under 18 are to be cared for in the event of your death. *Estate plans* are more nuanced, and detailed documents, which can have the additional benefit of minimizing some of the expenses associated with the transferring of assets and paying taxes. Estate plans also include your specific wishes around healthcare choices, end-of-life care, and specifies the person/s you want to administer the distribution of your assets.

The cost of administering a *trust* varies based upon the size of the estate, the state in which you live, and the complexity of the trust itself. Without a trust, *probating*—or the execution of a will—can take up to 5% of the total value of an estate and often takes longer, with an uncontested probate taking on average more than a year to complete. At present, the current federal estate tax exclusion is $5.45 million, with 19 states also imposing separate estate taxes. Estate plans can include creative ways to preserve assets for the next generation, such as "stretching" assets. This means setting up "stretch" distributions vs. a lump sum on investments such as IRAs for children or other beneficiaries. Estate plans are typically created by attorneys, the fees for creating and administering them are typically determined by them.

If and when you engage an attorney to create an estate plan for you, be sure to address the updating process and complete the paperwork to ensure all your accounts and the title to your property all specify the proper legal name of the trust. If you opt instead for a will, ensure your beneficiaries are named on your investments to avoid paying additional inheritance taxes.

Hildy's Story

When my father passed away in 2001, I worked with my mother to handle their living trust. I was shocked when the lawyers who set up the living trust for my parents initially wanted $35,000 to handle the paperwork to setup the bypass trust. This didn't seem right to me. My parents had already paid to have the trust set up—how could this be so costly? I consulted another attorney and moved my mother's estate planning to another law firm. Ultimately, the cost of settling all the legal and tax issues required was only $7,500. The difference was one firm was asking for a *percentage* of the estate and the other just charged an *hourly fee* to file all the paperwork. It pays to shop around and be aware of this percentage scam when you setup your living trust. ⊛

Financial Reflection

Please reflect upon the following questions:

What have you done to date around your financial retirement planning?

_____

_____

_____

_____

_____

_____

What do you imagine your lifestyle to be when you retire?

_____

_____

_____

_____

_____

_____

What're your specific worries or concerns about retirement savings?

_____

_____

_____

_____

_____

How many of your worries or concerns are grounded in emotion vs. facts?

_____

_____

_____

_____

_____

How might you modify your current living to reach your retirement goals?

_____

_____

_____

_____

_____

Is working part-time in retirement an option for you?

_____

_____

_____

_____

_____

Chapter 9

Health – Emotional and Physical Health

It is health that is real wealth and not pieces of gold and silver.

—Mahatma Gandhi

As you age, good health is everything. Doctor and hospital visits end up consuming so much of your time—even if you pay attention to your nutrition and exercise. According to experts at Northwestern Mutual, genetics account for just 20-30% of your projected longevity, with 70-80% of your longevity impacted by the choices you make about diet, exercise, smoking, and drinking, and other risk factors that affect overall health. While we're bombarded by messages of healthy living, we all have challenges to putting these messages into practice.

Stanford University's Palliative Care division recently reported, "Modern medicine has not only prolonged living but has also prolonged dying. Recent advances in biomedicine have converted grave illnesses like cancer into chronic illnesses. About 2 million Americans will die this year. Less than 10% of this population will experience a sudden or relatively rapid death due to cardiac diseases, trauma etc. Most will be diagnosed, live and endure life with a chronic illness for a prolonged period before transitioning into death. Improved sanitation, concerted efforts in public health and the development of advanced medical interventions have continued to increase life expectancies."

Biomedicine can't conquer death, but it has succeeded in prolonging life—even in cases of chronic illness. How might you adequately prepare for this transition and avoid being a negative statistic? Training for this transition is critical. Just as we might train for a special athletic event, so must we train for getting older. It might help to look at the following focus areas and consider your strengths and opportunities to address legacy health issues and build some new, healthier habits.

Bright Idea

The "Activities of Daily Living" are a set of activities used to evaluate an individual's ability to live on their own and are based on six criteria including bathing, dressing, toilet use, transferring (in and out of bed or a chair), continence, and eating.

Each criterion is graded on a level of dependence:

- Performs independently
- Performs with assistance
- Unable to perform.

Clinicians and social workers typically assign one point each for the ability to perform and use the results to create care plans for the individual. It's always important to get advice from a doctor who can assess how you're doing and provide medical advice on how to remain as strong and active as you can be as you age.

Bright Idea

What might you need to do differently as you consider your current state of fitness? Even if you aren't an athlete, just think of what it might mean to lose your hand strength, compromising your ability to open jars of food and cook for yourself. Think about how to lubricate your joints and get the synovial fluid moving so you can move without pain or difficulty. How will you avoid hip fractures, which are known as the "fast track" to the hospital, pneumonia, and then death?

To prevent hip fractures, clinicians suggest 1200 milligrams of supplemental calcium and 600 international units of Vitamin D to maintain healthy, dense bones. Additionally, it's helpful to do weight-bearing exercise such as walking, swimming, dancing, and weight training and practice yoga or Pilates to cultivate balance that typically deteriorates with age.

Smoking and excessive alcohol consumption can degrade bone density, which can also make you more susceptible to falling more readily. Special care should also be given to the home environment by removing potential hazards such as throw rugs, cords, or anything that you could trip on. It can also help to monitor your eyesight at least every other year to be vigilant about diabetes, which can cause low blood sugar cause unsteadiness on your feet. It's also important to be screened for other diseases that may impair the ability to see potential obstacles clearly.

Ann's Story

Every year, our water polo team attends the Bay Area Senior Games at Stanford University. This event offers mature athletes a chance to compete in a wide variety of sports including archery, cycling, lawn bowling, pickle ball, rugby, triathlon, and volleyball. Their mission is to promote healthy, active lifestyles for adults over the age of 50. It's very inspiring and energizing to see little children running around, wearing hand-made t-shirts that say, "Team Nana," and watch them cheer for their grandparents. ✹

Maintaining and Gaining Healthy Habits

What if you're more comfortable on the couch than in the saddle of a bike? It's never too late to build and reinforce healthy choices and best practices for re-orienting yourself to a healthier lifestyle. Tao Porchon-Lynch, certified by the Guinness Book of World records at age 96 as the world's oldest yoga teacher, shared her top 5 rules for a long, happy life:

- Don't procrastinate—tomorrow never comes.
- You can't believe in something if you only do it halfway.
- Each day, whatever is in your mind materializes.
- Never think about what can go wrong. I know my best day is every day.
- If you wait for something good to happen, it will. Don't look for tragedy.

Letting go of old habits and creating new ones is something that we may have been practicing our whole lives. Isn't it interesting to see how very challenging it is to stop the patterns of habituation, and how easy it is to fall back into old behaviors that no longer serve us?

To be sure, part of the challenge is physical, but so much of our resistance is rooted in our internalized self-talk. How many times have you made a commitment to go to the gym or go for a walk, only to talk yourself out of it? Holding a larger vision for a happier, healthier, more fit lifestyle is more useful than browbeating ourselves for our lapses, and ultimately will yield better results in the long run.

Here, we recommend using *appreciative inquiry*—an approach started by David Cooperrider—to invite positive change in instead of forcing it to happen. We can ask ourselves powerful questions to stimulate positive action, instead of critical, negative thoughts which can reinforce the opposite of our intentions. These questions might sound like:

- What physical activity would spark joy in my life?
- How would I feel if I mastered a new sport, or took up a new physical activity?

Ann's Story

My husband and I have made a game out of sharing some of the vagaries of aging. Like a houseguest you didn't expect, there are surprises that we've both encountered. I still remember finding my first big brown age spot and told him, "Surprise! I didn't know that was coming to live on my face!" To mitigate the negativity associated with some of these surprises, it's helped to focus on the things I'm grateful for as I continue to age. Marriage counselors know that for every statement of criticism or negativity, there needs to be an "offset" of 5 positive things to keep the relationship energy flowing. We apply this principle to our aging process, remembering a pillow in my parents' home that stated in bold embroidery, "Every Age Has Its Pleasures." With the advent of my brown spots, I thought how well they'll blend with my freckles, how much I now look like my beloved maternal grandmother, how lucky am I that it isn't skin cancer, how grateful I am that my husband loves me without a perfect complexion—and thank God for makeup! ✸

Observe Your Mental Health

Some of us might fare well with our physical well-being yet struggle with staying healthy emotionally. Some seniors may be happy as a clam, even as they become physically limited in their abilities. Of course, some seniors struggle with both mental and physical issues as they age. It's easy to understand the toll it takes on a physical body when we carry extra weight. But what about carrying around the weight of unfinished emotional business—like forgiving someone—or having the conversation you've always wanted to have, or speaking your truth? It's so easy to rationalize that this kind of extra weight isn't important, or that there's time to let these emotional wounds heal organically—but is that true? Aging can provide a galvanizing spark that's critical to seizing the moment and confronting emotions, situations, or longings that we've kept at bay or pushed down, in lieu of other priorities. Consider the health benefits of addressing what's long

- What would it feel like to be supported by others like me, trying a new health practice?

- Is there a choice I could make that would serve my health that I could incorporate gradually?

- How can I become more present in my body?

Hildy's Story

My brother was in his late 40s when he developed a cold and sore throat that lasted just way too long. He went to the doctor several times for routine treatments before his primary care provider suggested he see an ear nose and throat specialist. The specialist noticed a small growth in the very back of his throat, which after a biopsy, proved cancerous. Luckily, the doctor had caught it when it was small—he was able to have laser treatment for the tumor. My brother is now in his 60s and cancer-free. If he'd continued to ignore his symptoms—no matter how insignificant they may have seemed at the time—his cancer could've spread to other parts of his body, and his recovery might not have been as successful.

An esthetician friend swears that she can "see" skin cancer. She shared a story with me about one of her out-of-town clients, who came to see her. When she asked the client about a scratchy patch of skin, she said that she'd been to the doctor, who'd reassured her, "It's nothing." The esthetician encouraged her to seek out a second opinion—she did, and the second opinion confirmed it was a melanoma. Likewise, many hairdressers are also certified estheticians, and are trained to look for suspicious moles on their client's head and neck. If someone who can see parts of your body that you can't—or who routinely see parts of your body—note changes to you, it never hurts to make certain of what those changes might mean. Remember that even highly-trained physicians can miss a diagnosis or ignore/minimize your concerns—particularly in female-identified patients, or elderly patients— so it's helpful to be well-educated, proactive, and prepared for all medical visits. If you're shy to speak up, bringing along a partner or friend to advocate for you and help process information when it comes to more complex health issues can be an invaluable resource. ❀

Healthcare Year at a Glance

Practice	Jan	Feb	Mar	Apr	May	June	Jul	Aug	Sep	Oct	Nov	Dec
Primary Care												
Dentist												
Eye Doctor												
Dermatologist												
Audiologist												
Physical Therapist												
Chiropractor												
Cardiologist												
Orthopedist												
Neurologist												

Health Year At a Glance Exercise

You can download Encore exercise from our website at https://yourencoreteam.com/ . Use this blank template to keep track of your yearly appointments in one place.

Organizing an annual year-at-a-glance calendar can help to provide peace of mind, as well as to ensure nothing slips through the cracks. You can you use your online electronic medical record to help you keep track. This can be extremely helpful for people living alone.

been on your emotional "To-Do" list, and you'll be amazed at the positive impact this could have on your emotional health.

Sometimes, emotional wellbeing isn't something you can easily fix on your own. Clinical depression and other biochemically-rooted mental illnesses require expert intervention, behavioral changes, and sometimes, even medical therapy. The National Alliance of Mental Illness (NAMI) statistics place approximately 1 in 5 adults in the US—43.8 million, or 18.5%—as managing some form of mental illness. Because of the stigma that still surrounds mental health issues, building awareness and compassion of how they present and their impact on aging adults is key. Depression affects more than 6.5 million of the 35 million Americans aged 65 years or older. According to the NAMI, fewer than 50% of senior Americans with mental health issues receive the services they need, and face a compounded stigma of both aging and mental illness. There's a need and growing demand for services to address their needs, with a limited and sporadic availability of social workers and mental health clinicians to serve senior patients. There's shortage of mental health professionals, and to make things even more difficult, many seniors refuse to acknowledge there's even a problem.

Seniors, as a demographic, are often more socially isolated, and because of this, there can be a missing feedback loop from the outside world indicating the onset or acceleration of a mental health issue or crisis. Human body chemistry changes over time, which can trigger previously dormant chemical imbalances in the brain. Jane Pauley, a 30-year television news veteran, was diagnosed with *hypomania* (Bipolar 3), triggered by a combination on antidepressants and steroids prescribed to treat a bad case of hives.

Mental health expert Dr. Dilip Jeste, who focuses his work on older adults, advocates for early prevention as opposed to just the treatment of depressive episodes. Especially following a heart attack, cardiac event, or a stroke, it becomes increasingly important to monitor yourself of your loved ones for signs of depression, as these times of physical trauma can be "triggering events" which flood the brain's chemistry with responsive hormones, chemicals, and can create imbalances which manifest as mental health issues. It's imperative to be open, honest, and non-judgemental with both family and health care providers if there are concerns about a senior's mental health and well-being.

Dr. Jeste also advocates for *the positive psychiatry of aging*, an approach that seeks positive outcomes in aging individuals with mental illness, and takes into account the positive psychological factors associated with recovery such as resilience, optimism, social engagement, and wisdom. Dr. Jeste endeavors to redefine what constitutes successful aging, considering specifically at the attributes of thoughtful decision-making, empathy, compassion, altruism, emotional stability, self-understanding, decisiveness, and tolerance for divergent values and their potential biological roots. As you enter your Encore phase, make note of your mental attitudes and observe changes to your own reaction and behaviors to people and situations. Be sure to note any changes, because even if they're not readily apparent to you, these changes might be indicative of depression or declining mental capacity. Be your own first-person observer of your behavior, and ask your friends to help you if they notice significant changes in your personality, behavior, hygiene, or ability to engage with the world.

Dealing with Hospitalization

Despite our most fervent wishes that we remain hale and hearty—both emotionally and physically—there's no escaping our mortality. Experts report that only 20% of people die in our sleep, peacefully and at home. A recent study published by the Journal of the American Medical Association (JAMA) found that in 2009, 33.5% of Medicare beneficiaries died at home, 24.9% died in the hospital, and about 42% died in hospice care. In order to return home, specialized support may be needed in the form of home health workers, traveling nurses, palliative care, or even hospice care.

For many families, a family member provides the caregiving. In 2013, about 40 million family caregivers in the United States performed 37 billion hours of care for older adults with limitations, based on their ability to perform basic routines of self-care. According to another recent study, this amounts to approximately $470 billion of unpaid labor.

Have a Health Advocate

Because the majority of healthcare happens through conversation, it's all too easy to miss key parts of what was said—and even more importantly—the nuances. While patients will often receive an after-care visit summarization, it can also help to digitally record the actual interactions with your clinician on your phone or with a dedicated recording device. That way, it's almost as though you have a second pair of ears. This is important when your health is compromised and you have trouble following the conversation, or if you have hearing issues. While a friend may be able to join you for a simple clinic or primary care visit, it might be necessary at some point to hire a health advocate.

Health Advocates—sometime called *Patient Advocates*—organize, manage, and educate their clients on health care needs, recommended procedures or courses of treatment, and their associated costs. Some health advocates are licensed clinicians such as nurses, nursing assistants, or nurse practitioners focusing on coordination of numerous caregivers and specialists, while others are former social workers focused on helping patients in hospital or assisted-cares facilities. Health advocates understand the nuances of the ever-changing world of healthcare, and can help seniors by alleviating frustration, offering proactive ideas, and providing reassurance that all aspects of an individual's care are being properly addressed. This can be especially helpful for those patients with complex care needs.

Defining the term *complex care* has been an ongoing challenge for the healthcare industry, as each patient is unique and requires specific forms of healthcare to successfully their address unique needs. The complexity of care isn't simply relegated to physical health—there may also be issues of mental health, social, or financial challenges connected to a person's health issues. Most experts agree, however, that the most common and costly chronic health conditions include asthma, diabetes, heart failure, obesity, and depression, which, if untreated or managed improperly, can cause recurrent or frequent hospitalizations.

Care Options as You Age

Your needs for health care support change as you age—knowing *when* to employ the right professional is something you must continually assess—don't just assume that a family member or friend will be able to perform all the care you'll need. Selecting the right care provider at the right time requires a realistic and rigorous assessment of what's needed, education and identification of possible solutions, and a comprehensive screening process. The most important qualities of healthcare excellence include *communication, critical thinking, patience, adaptability*, and *attentiveness*. What are the differences in the kind of care you'll need, as you near the end of your life?

The chart below outlines the type of support that's available and when you should consider accessing it, as well as outlining the many ways you might approach your healthcare, especially at the end of your life.

Support	Fits when...
Online Communities	Need to connect with others with similar health challenges or concerns, but not a substitute for professional screenings and expertise. Need to hear about other's journey with an illness like yours.
Home Health Care	Difficult to complete the ADL (Activities of Daily Living).
Visiting Nurse	Person needs home health, palliative, or hospice care. Can be especially helpful for aging individuals with disabilities. Resources and more information can be found at the Visiting Nurses of America Association. http://www.vnaa.org/
Gerontologist	Person has multiple chronic needs with complex medical or social needs that are impacting their health. Gerontologist or Primary Care Physician can receive POLST (Physician Orders for Life-sustaining Treatments) which complement an Advance Care Directive but also cover artificially administered nutrition and are actual doctor's orders which can't be ignored like Advanced Care Directives or DNRs.
Social Worker	Individual needs help with meal delivery, rides, and opportunities for specialized support (e.g., grief groups for people who have lost a spouse).
Palliative Care	There is a need for pain management either within a hospital setting or at home. Team will use the Braden pain scale to assess pain and manage it to prevent the person from feeling "fuzzy."
Hospice Care	Person is within 6 months of dying; Medicare may cover costs for hospice care.

Writer Susan Sontag asked her son to be her healthcare advocate. Despite his personal wish to alleviate her suffering by discontinuing painful bone marrow treatment when she was battling her third incidence of cancer, he held steadfast to her wishes to do *everything* to prolong her life. This is one way in which your healthcare advocate acts on your behalf and honors your wishes—regardless of what they want for you. You may want to have your advocate listen, take notes, and then later, compare their notes with you to ensure what they heard and what you heard are in sync, which can help reconcile any differences and clarify the next appropriate steps. Innovations in telemedicine and video visits mean that these interactions can be supported by technology with playback capabilities. Medication adherence and compliance with the physician's orders improve when there's someone invested in your well-being. The pace, demands, and shift changes clinicians experience can impact the quality and clarity of their interactions with patients. You can also concentrate on healing instead of worrying if you have someone by your side that can advocate for you and your unique needs. Some hospitals, realizing the importance of patient advocates, have a pool of volunteers who can support a patient through the ER, Admissions, and length of their stay in the hospital.

It's critical to enlist the support of a trusted partner, friend, or relative to act as a proactive healthcare advocate. It's also helpful to discuss mutual expectations when asking someone to be your trusted healthcare advocate and to clarify how major decisions will be made (e.g., shared decision-making, decision always made by the patient, etc.) Before initiating such a conversation, it can be helpful to carefully reflect on what you want, why you want it, and how to best share these expectations with your chosen advocate. Last—but not least—be sure to record what you each agree to uphold and add these agreements and other pertinent wishes around your health and end of life requests to an official document, which you should then notarize and keep with all your legal papers.

Bright Idea

The best days to seek admittance to long-term care facilities are Monday through Thursday, during the day shifts. While admission to a nursing home doesn't require a physician's order, payment by Medicare or Medicaid requires a physician's referral.

Cultural and Generational Considerations

In healthcare, there's an acknowledged disparity between how people from different genders, cultures, socioeconomic classes, and generations access and experience healthcare. People in lower-income areas generally face more obstacles to getting their primary healthcare needs met. They may not have access to insurance plans or a primary physician located in their community. In some cases, this lack of access results in the Emergency Room becoming a primary source of healthcare. This disparity only intensifies when it comes to retiring, dying, end-of-life decisions, and death. Not only are there variations in how the individual experiencing retirement and end-of-life issues processes and adapts to them, but there are also behaviors and beliefs of the care team to contend with as well.

At the center of these systems is a person's end-of-life decisions. Experts report that religion and tradition are the largest factors in family decision-making, noting significant cultural differences in how issues of death and dying vary. For example, for many Latin communities, the removal of a person from life support can be perceived as tantamount to killing them, so reaching a familial consensus is the most important factor influencing end-of-life decisions.

Conversely, in many Cambodian families, these decisions are often delegated to the spouse or children alone, whereas many Hindu communities believe that when a person dies, their soul simply moves from one body to the next on its path to reach heaven (nirvana), so there's less of a pull to prolong life. Complicating these cultural divides are what's collectively called the *prac-*

tice patterns of the care team, their training, and *their* personal beliefs, which are internalized and ultimately manifest in the way caregivers interact with and serve their patients.

Many proactive healthcare leaders now offer coursework, training, and continuing education in culturally-competent care, hoping to make healthcare more inclusive and sensitive to the needs of divergent cultures. Clinicians are becoming better trained to ask vital questions and to practice compassionate listening, to support their patients and their families, while respecting their traditions and beliefs. Whatever your cultural or religious background, it's important for you to be aware of any potential internalized biases in your care team or your family when you consider who you choose as your health advocate. Be sure to question your care team—especially if you think they may not understand your wishes for your end-of-life care. There's never any harm in making sure everyone's on the same page!

Reflections

What are your physical and emotional health strengths?

_____

_____

_____

_____

_____

What are the specific opportunities you have to improve your emotional and/or physical health?

_____

_____

_____

_____

_____

_____

What legacy health behaviors no longer support you, and what new behaviors do you want to practice?

_____

_____

_____

_____

What signs do you monitor to ensure you get the proper screenings, healthcare, and nutrition as you age?

_____

_____

_____

_____

_____

_____

Who'll be your proactive health advocate, and have they accepted your request and discussed mutual expectations?

_____

_____

_____

_____

_____

_____

What's your family's belief system around dying and death?

_____

_____

_____

_____

_____

_____

How do you want to communicate your needs to your care team (e.g., family meeting, written document supporting your DNR, POLST, etc.?)?

_____

_____

_____

_____

_____

_____

Who do you want to make your end-of-life decision, and what'll you do if you change your mind?

_____

_____

_____

_____

_____

_____

Chapter 10

Spirituality

The further the spiritual evolution of mankind advances, the more certain it seems to me that the path to genuine religiosity does not lie through the fear of life, and the fear of death, and blind faith, but through striving after rational knowledge.

—Albert Einstein

Seeking Meaning and Purpose in Life and Death

The Theosophical Society in America's mission is the open-minded inquiry into world's religions, philosophy, science, and the arts to understand the divine wisdom of the ages. This organization defines *spirituality* as, "...a broad concept, with room for many perspectives. In general, it includes a sense of connection to something bigger than us, and typically involves a search for meaning in life. As such, it's a universal human experience—something that touches us all." Taking a comprehensive look at spirituality in the context of contemplating your own mortality means making larger connections between the universal human experience and ourselves. It can include asking powerful questions about how your life has made a difference— for ourselves, for others, and for the world. Unpacking the baggage around this highly-charged topic requires taking stock of your thoughts, feelings, and utilizing the gift of reflection.

According to Kokua Mau, a Palliative Care organization in Hawaii, people who are experiencing the process of dying want reassurance of the following things:

- Things they were once responsible for will be taken care of
- Friends and loved ones will be okay without them

- All is forgiven

- Their life had meaning

- They will be remembered

It sometimes feels as though everything in the Westernized American culture conspires against people taking the time to pause, reflect, and assess whether we're living a purposeful life. Our days tend to be filled to the brim with the activity of daily living and the additional challenge of navigating the virtual world by staying connected to work, friends, family, and events happening all over the globe on a 24/7 basis.

Many people nowadays go to sleep with their phones right next to them—so they can grab them immediately upon waking up. While staying connected electronically has opened up a world of new possibilities, it's been at the cost of often feeling like the virtual world trumps the person in front of you, and has created the "celebrification" of our culture (in which each person wants to be viewed as a celebrity), one where every minute detail of your life needs to be posted for others to consume.

The challenge, then, is to quiet your mind and find time away from what distracts you from doing the important work of getting in touch with your true essence as a unique human being. Defining your purpose in life can feel uncomfortable—daunting, to say the least. Unlike most other animals on this planet, humans have the ability to contemplate our death and the losses of those we love. Though we push aside and deny the fact of our mortality, we often forget that it can also be a galvanizing force to explore who we are, how we're connected to something bigger than ourselves, and how we can continue to live the best way possible until we die.

Fear of Death

Fear of death is a constant of the human condition. Intellectually, we all know that we'll die, but emotionally, our egos are resistant to acknowledging this. Freud noted the ultimate paradox of this, as he grappled with his own terminal cancer: "The aim of life is death… [yet] we cannot observe our own death." He believed that the competing goals of the *id* (pleasure), the *ego* (reality), and the *superego* (morality) and their relentless struggle for dominance is the struggle resulting in a person's internal conflict. This conflict produces *anxiety*. The *ego*, which functions as a mediator between the two extremes of the *id* and the *superego*, attempts to reduce this anxiety by using defense mechanisms. Denial is one of key defense mechanisms, so you might say that the denial of death is the *ultimate* defense mechanism.

Xenophobia—the fear of the unknown—comes from the Greek word, *xenos*, meaning foreigner or stranger, and *phobos*, meaning morbid fear. Death is both foreign and strange, so it makes sense that it inspires fear. Some of us may fear death itself, some of us may fear being forgotten after living a life that didn't matter, some of us fear losing everything we've known or cared about, and some of us may fear all of these things more—and more. Being open and honest with ourselves about what we fear *specifically* about death takes courage, time, patience, honesty, self-reflection, and most of all—love. It can help to have a partner or to participate in a group as you explore the root cause of your fears and take proactive steps to deal with those fears. Therapy, meditation, journaling, guided exercises, and silent retreats are other helpful tools you might use to explore your fears and achieve a more peaceful perspective.

Ann's Story

Over a lunch date whose conversation explored a wide range of heavy topics, a friend and I tried an experiment. We challenged ourselves to write about some of the things that we'd just talked about, with the intention of synthesizing the information and applying it to how we were actually living our lives. It was a wonderful experience, so we now meet on a regular basis, have lunch, discuss what it means to be alive, to live and love well, and how to deal with changing relationships. Then, we pull out our notebooks and come up with a writing prompt, a leading question, or set of words that best reflects the tenor of our most recent conversation. We then do a timed writing exercise, and share what we've written with each other. This writing date has proven to be a powerful balm for both of our souls, helping to clarify things we've each been struggling with about death, spirituality, and how to live a more meaningful life. Since that first lunch-and-writing date, we've compiled a lot of personal writings, which we can refer to when wrestling with a difficult situation or a tough day, and we both agree that we find both the process and the outputs very comforting. ⊛

Hildy's Story

As he was dying of leukemia, my father would joke, "Don't be sad. Remember nobody gets out of here alive!" He maintained a positive outlook on his own mortality, certain he would see his parents, brother, and friends who had preceded him in death. Educated by the Jesuits, he was a faithful, life-long Catholic who wasn't afraid of death, because his faith was such that heaven awaited him. When we turned 25, he joked, "You're young for your first 25 years, middle-aged from 25 to 50, old from 50 to 75, and after that you're on borrowed time." ⊛

People have always been naturally curious about death and dying, and the internet has made it easier for these people to connect to each other, often through coordinated online events like the Death Expo, Dying Matters Awareness Week, and the growing popularity of movements such as Death Cafés and The Conversation Project. These death-oriented events, movements, and organizations connect people who want to honor and explore end-of-life experiences, death, and bereavement. Though to some, this may all seem a little macabre, remember that death is a natural part of living, and none of these events glorify death so much as they honor it as simply an unexplored extension of life.

The Death Expo is targeted to clinicians, business, grassroots organizations, and lay people. Death Cafés and The Conversation are geared specifically to provide a way for people to come together, share, explore, and learn from others about the mysteries of dying and death. Hospice doctors and nurses or health care workers often host Death Cafés in local bookstores, coffee shops, libraries, or even hospitals. The events are organized as unstructured and open conversations with strangers where people are encouraged to break into small groups to share their experiences with death without judgment or seeking or giving advice. Participants are free to share their personal experiences, how they've experienced the loss of a loved one, their grief or bereavement, and to work through their search for meaning around death and life. At the end, each group shares what they've learned with the other groups. The topics vary based on who's participating, and how much each small group connects with one another, and can be amazingly positive and very informative. It can also be comforting to connect with others and know that you aren't alone in wondering about or trying to make sense of all the unknowns around death and dying.

The Conversation Project was founded by Ellen Goodman, a project offering resources and toolkits on their website supporting open and honest discussions with loved ones about how you want to spend your last days. It's especially helpful if you're having difficulty making plans with aging parents and loved ones who don't want to have the conversation about their death. They offer a set of downloadable documents, intended to be a guide for initiating difficult conversations around Alzheimer's disease, how to talk with your doctor about end-of-life care, and even more specialized documents for parents dealing with their children's end-of-life care. In addition to a blog, they also offer resources for community organizations to host events and conversations about death and dying—so if there isn't an event near you, you could be the change you want to see in your community by hosting one.

Having "The Conversation"—both to clarify and share what you want, need, and hope for during the end of life—is a very powerful act. Piercing the veil of silence around your deeply held beliefs, wishes, and hopes is itself an act of empowerment and vulnerability, one which can create deeper intimacy and peace within yourself and in your relationships with friends and loved ones. Mindfulness about death—like mindfulness about living—doesn't always come naturally. We can practice having these conversations with friends or in a safe environment that isn't emotionally-charged before broaching The Conversation with family and loved ones.

One could argue that the internet and global community of connectedness has removed many of the social and cultural taboos and stigmas about death—whatever the reason, there are more resources available, and resources that are easier to access, than ever before. Steve Jobs, before he died of pancreatic cancer at 54, applied the creativity which had paved the way for so much success at Apple to his own death with his 2005 Stanford speech, "How to Live Before You Die," a reflection of vulnerability, courage, and dignity in the face of a terminal diagnosis. He shared with the 2005 graduates his practice of reminding himself daily that he would die, and how he used that as reminder to live as richly, deeply, and well as possible, noting that death—the ultimate "change agent"—always gets rid of the old to invite in the new.

Bright Idea

Having a sense of humor can help break down some of your internalized resistance. The book *Exit Laughing: How Humor Takes the Sting Out of Death* offers stories about how humor can help soothe and heal in times of grief and loss. From the story of four friends with all their identification locked safely in the car, trapped in a mental hospital after their friend's wake to a husband commiserating over the death of a grandmother, when it was actually her *cat* who'd died to a hearse driver who gets lost and leads a caravan of mourners into a neighborhood of unsuspecting families, the stories are a reminder that laughter, like death, is a natural part of our humanity, and that in times of great sorrow, sometimes a laugh can be the thing that helps up get through one minute to the next.

Rituals for the Mind, Body & Spirit

Consider the rituals of death—who benefits from them the most? The person dying, their living friends and family, or both? Theologian Tom Driver notes, "Rituals are primarily instruments designed to change a situation." What bigger change is there than death? If religion or faith is a part of your life, your survivors may have a clear blueprint to follow for the rituals to perform at your death. Most organized religions—churches, mosques, temples, and synagogues—have some form of ritual, often handed down from generation to generation over time.

Consider how some faiths approach death in their ceremonies: Catholicism has a sacrament called the "Anointing of the Sick," which the ailing and elderly can receive on a regular basis from a priest. One of Judaism's basic tenets is that no dying person should be left alone, so a rabbi may be asked to join with friends and family to pray. Many Seventh-Day Adventists believe death to be an unconscious sleep, nothing to be fearful of, so family members and friends will visit and offer sympathy to the family as their loved ones are dying. In many forms of Hinduism, family members and spiritual leaders will gather to sing and read from sacred texts, and also may opt to tie a thread around the wrist and neck of the dying person, sprinkle water from the Ganges on them, or place a sprig of the sacred basil bush on their tongue. These are just a few examples of religious rituals that are often performed as a person is dying, and for many, these rituals and ceremonies are a source of great comfort, serve to ease some of the fear and anxiety of death, and help family and friends grieve together.

For those who are more secular, agnostic, or atheistic in their beliefs, considering rituals at the end of life outside of the parameters of religion may also provide some unique opportunities to be creative and embrace what's provided comfort during their lives. While it is common for people who've moved away from the religion they were raised in to move back to its rituals during their later phases of life, this is not an absolute, and there's much to be said for a person creating their own traditions. Creating your own rituals can be a sacred act, unbounded by traditional, religious expectations that provides much comfort to you as well as the person or people with whom you're experiencing these rituals.

Dying Rituals can focus on any combination of soothing the dying person's body, mind, and/or spirit. Ways to attend to the dying person's body and spirit might include spraying lavender to freshen their face while reminding them with specific examples of how much joy they've created and shared with others. You might massage their hands gently with scented cream while saying thank you for all the love and work their hands produced. For a body struggling to hang onto life while suffering terribly, you can rub your hands to warm them up, and then gently place them over the dying person's heart and whisper to them that it's okay to let go.

In rituals to attend to the dying person's mind, careful consideration of the dying person's present state of mind is of paramount importance, as there can be dramatic shifts from one day to another, one moment to another. While our reptilian brain knows how to die just as it knows how to live, it's our *limbic* or mammalian brain that activates fear, feeding, or fighting as a means of self-preservation and therefore may be holding on tight even though the body is ready to go. Even writer Susan Sontag—who fiercely vowed to fight death with everything she had—vacillated in her final days between stoicism and softening to the soothing comfort her beloved friends were offering. She loved writing, which she lovingly called "the work," observing human nature through penning essays, watching movies, and reading as her chosen rituals to usher her final transition from life to death. Regardless of a person's religious or spiritual beliefs, any combination of poetry, music, stories, prayers, or meditation can be incorporated as rituals to support dying.

Ann's Story

I once traveled to Ghana to meet our younger daughter there after she'd spent a semester studying in Accra. I was intrigued by the culture as a whole, but what struck me most were the funerals—which typically cost more than weddings—and were often advertised on billboards, held on

Saturdays to allow as many people as possible to arrive in the traditional black or red funeral clothing of the culture to eat, drink, listen to music, and dance in celebration of the person who had died.

By mistake, we wandered into a woodworking shop where workers carved and painted beautiful coffins in stunning shapes and vibrant colors. These coffins are made to the specifications of the bereaved family, often reflecting the deceased's career or favorite things in life. We saw a corncob for a farmer, a camera for a photographer, and an airplane for a pilot. They were beautiful, and made to represent the life of the person as they were ushered into death. During my visit to the woodshop, I purchased a 3-foot urn in the shape of a Coke bottle, which has a secret compartment for ashes. Though to some, this might seem a macabre souvenir, but to me, it's more of a *memento mori,* a reminder to poke fun at death—where you can. ❁

Prayer Circles around the dying person are other end-of-life rituals valued for the comfort offered to both the dying person and the loved ones left behind. Prayer circles can be as simple as a family or friends coming together to hold hands around the dying person's bed and sharing a simple wish for the person dying, or they can be more structured, often led by an officiant using traditional prayers or sacred rites for the dying. Perform a simple internet search and you can even find virtual prayer circles, where you can sign up to pray for a specific person who's actively dealing with a terminal illness or is in the process of dying.

Some religions implement a *cleansing of the chakras* ritual for the dying person, a rite intended to prepare their spirit for the transition. In certain faiths, *chakras* are viewed as the key energy reservoirs of the body, able to influence the health and wellness of our mind, body, and spirits. There are seven chakras, each of which correspond to a specific area of the body, and for those who ascribe to this system of belief, it's difficult to feel peaceful when the chakras are out of balance. Once the person has died, there's an additional ritual of *disengaging the chakras,* which ideally happens within 40 hours of death, and helps to usher their spirit on to the next phase of their existence.

End-of-life rituals—religious or secular—can help a person not only to experience a peaceful death, but also a sacred one, bringing reconciliation and acceptance to the loved ones as well as to the person dying. Rituals help to heal the pain of letting go, while concurrently connecting us with something much greater than our earthly concerns. Despite the comfort rituals provide, remember that rituals aren't meant to take the place of medical or hospice care. Their practice assumes that the physical needs of the dying person are well attended to and that pain management is under control.

Threshold Choirs

In many communities, you can contact a Threshold Choir. These volunteers will come to the bedside of a dying person and sing soothing songs in three-part harmony. Threshold Choirs are a free volunteer service performed by caring members of the community, who offer the gift of song as a comfort to both the person dying and their family.

Hildy's Story

When my father was in the hospital dying and my last sibling had finally arrived from out of town, my mother, my siblings, our spouses, and I all gathered around his bed in a circle. He was a devout, life-long Catholic, wearing a suit to mass every Sunday out of respect for the church— even in the hottest summer months. To honor my dad and usher him through his passage, we circled his bed, holding hands and reciting the "Our Father" and "Hail Mary" prayers in unison, as a family. This memory will always bring me to tears—the ritual was my mother's idea, the perfect way to say goodbye to such a great man, in way that he would appreciate. ✸

Bright Idea

Dying rituals can be incorporated into your personal **Death Plan**. Consider creating a list of rituals you might find comforting to cultivate peace during the dying process. In a later chapter, we'll expand more creating a death plan that you'd like to follow including things like what kind of memorial you might want, what to do with your remains and how to distribute your assets. Dying rituals are a part of this plan. There's no right or wrong ritual, as long as it's fully focused on the person, their specific needs at that moment, and carried out with love and tenderness. Using the Agency for Human Dignity framework of **Five Wishes** can also be helpful in creating your **Dying Rituals**. The Five Wishes is a popular, easy-to-read living will, written in simple language, intended to affirm and safeguard the dignity of humans as they age. It's easy to find online and download into a hard copy format, so that a person's specific wishes can about their end of life decisions can be captured clearly and succinctly, creating greater peace of mind of the person and those committed to honoring their wishes.

Ideas to Create Comforting Rituals for Your Mind, Body, and Spirit:

- Reflect upon what has comforted you in childhood during times of worry or pain
- Incorporate what has most deeply nourished you in your life
- Incorporate special family traditions, stories, rituals, and photographs
- Consider your preferences around lighting, scent, objects, the power of silence, readings, prayer, and touch.

Ann's Story

It was difficult to be a bystander while my mother was actively engaged in her losing battle with lung cancer, watching every agonizing, gasping, rasping breath helplessly. Little by little, she shifted from our shared world to a kind of "never-never land,"—she could hear us, but ultimately she stopped talking, stopped heaving, and her body finally started to let go. She'd chosen to die in the liminal time between night and day, waiting until the room had emptied of family members and the sharing of family stories and taking pictures of each of our hands holding hers had wound down.

We arrived at the hospital at 4:00 a.m., never having seen a dead person before. Spontaneously, we invented some soothing rituals for ourselves, to guide us through the complicated feelings of having been left behind. One of my sisters took a handful of dried lavender that she'd brought with her, using the petals to make a heart on our mother's chest. Then, we each took one of the beautiful yellow roses another of my sisters had brought, and laid them on our mother's body, giving her a final goodbye kiss. Though not rooted in tradition, these spontaneous rituals helped us feel the closure we'd hoped to experience by being in the room with her when she died. ⊛

Hildy's Story

When my father died, my mother was sitting at his bedside. She's described seeing what she perceived as a "wave of energy," which started at the top of my dad's head and rippled down to his feet—and then he was gone. She believes what she saw was his soul leaving his body— and who's to say that she's not right?

When my good friend Dylia's mother died, Dylia was cuddled up in bed next to her, and described a feeling of an unstoppable energy wave that crossed over her—something *felt* but not *seen*. These end-of-life experiences provided comfort to the both my mother and to Dylia, re-affirming their belief that death doesn't fully take away our loved ones, but that they instead move on to a better place, providing the hope that we may actually see them again. ✸

Dying Rituals Exercise

You can download Encore exercise from our website at

https://yourencoreteam.com/

Dying Rituals

What comforted you as a child?

_____

_____

_____

_____

_____

What sensory additions do you prefer?

_____

_____

_____

_____

_____

_____

What nourishes you now?

_____

_____

_____

_____

_____

Are there family traditions you could use?

_____

_____

_____

_____

_____

_____

Reflection

What are my spiritual beliefs?

_____

_____

_____

_____

_____

How might they help or hinder my final transition?

_____

_____

_____

_____

_____

Who might I share my feelings about death and dying?

_____

_____

_____

_____

_____

What's the best way for me to process uncomfortable or scary feelings? (For example, write, talk, create, art, meet up with a friend, time in nature, garden, cook, etc.)

_____

_____

_____

_____

_____

_____

What kind of rituals might I want to create for myself when I'm dying, and how will I communicate my wishes?

_____

_____

_____

_____

_____

_____

Chapter 11

Legacy

What's it all about Alfie, is it just for the moment we live?

– Burt Bacharach

As Boomers begin to retire after decades of striving, many can now pause and ask the question Dionne Warwick belted out in the 60s: *What's it all about?* Maybe you've been asking this question all along—but most of us have been so busy living our lives that we haven't taken the time to consider our entire story arc. Here, we ask you to think more deeply about this question. Consider your purpose in life, what you've achieved, who's helped you along the way, how you'd like to be remembered. Could future generations benefit from what you've learned on your journey?

It's your Encore—what else do you want to experience before your final exit, stage left?

Share Your Experience

Your legacy is multi-faceted—if you have children, maybe your immediate thoughts are of how you might secure the future of your family. We invite you to revisit the chapter on **Money** if you're interested in how to preserve your family assets. But you know the saying—money isn't everything. There are so many things that define a person's legacy for you to consider. A life is made up of so many different parts, and your legacy can touch upon some, many, or all of these different moving parts. Ask yourself:

What are the defining notes of your life?

How will you document your wisdom, your memories, your triumphs and failures?

What knowledge can you impart?

What are the stories that only you can tell—and how do you want to share those stories?

Hildy's Story

My mother Marjorie — a nonagenarian — has a cherished family recipe for Irish scone. The secret of the recipe isn't in the ingredients themselves, but instead, it's in *how* the ingredients are mixed. There's a specific feel to the dough when the baker adds in just the right amount of buttermilk. Too much—the scone is flat. Too little—the scone will crumble. The scone comes out best when it's baked in seasoned cast iron pan that can fit in the oven. Our family cuts a holy cross into the dough, to give the scone a blessing, which also has the practical quality of letting some steam out while baking so the scone rises. A light dusting of flour on top is the final act of love before the baker pops it in the oven. This is the kind of practical, hands-on knowledge that isn't usually written down, but rather, is passed down through generations in the *doing*—the kind of knowledge that it would be such a shame to lose. If I'd just read my mother's scone recipe as it's written down, I would never be able to reproduce the same scone. Making it *with* her is what revealed all the subtleties of the recipe, little tricks she'd learned over a lifetime of making this particular recipe. Now, I've gained this secret, generational knowledge and can pass it on to my daughter, and she to her children, and so the recipe lives on—long after the original baker. ⊛

Bright Idea

Your mobile phone is a portable video studio; capable of recording, preserving, and sharing the knowledge you want to share with future generations on social media.

You might want to publish all your wisdom; recipes, stories, old poems, photos in a book format with simple to use tools. Create your content online and print out multiple copies for the loved ones you're leaving behind. What a great gift for children or grandchildren! You might think about periodic posting to social media like Pinterest, Instagram or Facebook. A recipe and story a week with pictures and voice annotation could reach a broader audience with your permission beyond your immediate social circle. Check out Legacy Boxes. Simply submit your memories in whatever format and they'll digitize them for you!

The old-school approach is to write your own autobiography or memoir for posterity sake. There are numerous resources to provide the structure and guidance to both initiate and complete this kind of project; check out local community colleges, private classes offered locally, and online courses through University extension or other institutes of learning.

Reflection

Consider these questions, and answer them—without judging yourself. Circle the questions are harder for you to answer.

- What defining moments have you had in your life?
- What have you learned from your greatest failures?
- Who was essential to the plot of your story?
- What verbal stories of your ancestors need to be written, recorded, or retold?
- What awards and honors throughout your life/career are you proud of that maybe your family doesn't even know about?
- What regrets do you have?
- What was the road not taken for you?

Think about the answers to these questions above as fuel for the story of your own personal journey. Think of this part of your life as the transformational story arc of a great play with three acts—the Early Years, the Middle Years and your *Encore*. This book is focused on the transformation stage from Retirement to Death that we like to call the Encore. The hard work of your younger years is done—but the climax and transformational moments are still to come.

If you choose to write the story of your life now, you may benefit from a phenomenon called the Observer effect: "In science, the term observer effect refers to changes that the act of observation will make on a phenomenon being observed." Just trying to put your story down on paper will likely make you look at your choices and behavior patterns, through which, you'll gain invaluable insights. Writing the Story of You is a valuable self-reflection exercise to do at any point in your life, but especially so as you near your Encore stage. You still have time to accomplish goals, make amends, set things right, and leave nothing undone—before you lack the energy or health to create new endings.

Living Your Life's Purpose?

If you still don't feel you're living your life's purpose, it's never too late. People who live to be centenarians have one thing in common—they still have passion in their life. It might be a physical activity that keeps you young—like tango dancing, biking, scuba diving, yoga, or travel. If you have health or physical limitations—or just prefer more low-key activities—you might consider reading, knitting, singing with a choir, learning a musical instrument, or other endeavors that bring meaning and purpose to your life. You might also consider sharing your passions through blogging or joining online groups, activities that be a source of comfort, connection, and purpose to your day-to-day life.

Bright Idea

Consider the wisdom of the aged. Here are some words of wisdom, collected in a blog of 100 Pieces of Advice from Centenarians:

- *Don't look at the calendar. Just keep celebrating every day.*
- *Invest in quality pieces; they never go out of style.*
- *I make myself go out every day, even if it's only to walk around the block. The key to staying young is to keep moving.*
- *Fall in love, get married. Sex is to be encouraged.*
- *Don't ever give up on love.*
- *Nobody else controls you.*
- *Make time to cry.*

Are you a late bloomer? Grandma Moses, a renowned American Folk Artist, began painting at 78. Colonel Sanders started the KFC franchise at age 65, going on to become a late-stage multimillionaire. Former President Jimmy Carter has served as an Honorary Chair for the World Justice project and built homes with Habitat for Humanity, arguably being of more service since his presidency ended, than while holding the most important job title of his life. During your *Encore*, you may have the time and energy to reinvent yourself and/or expose that you truly are at the core of your being. Thinking about your legacy is one way to delve into whether you've led the life you wanted to, and if you're leaving the world better than it was when you were born.

 **Reflection**

How will I be remembered if I died today?

_____

_____

_____

_____

_____

_____

How would I like to be remembered?

_____

_____

_____

_____

_____

_____

What steps will I take to close the gap in my desired legacy?

_____

_____

_____

_____

_____

_____

Do I have any unfinished business including;

Places to see?

_____

_____

_____

_____

_____

_____

Wrongs to right?

_____

_____

_____

_____

_____

_____

Debts to pay?

_____

_____

_____

_____

_____

_____

Skills to learn?

_____

_____

_____

_____

_____

Stories to share?

_____

_____

_____

_____

Objects to gift?

_____

_____

_____

_____

Who do I need to forgive?

_____

_____

_____

_____

Who do I need forgiveness from?

_____

_____

_____

_____

_____

_____

Bright Idea

You can write letters to let important people in your life know what they've meant to you. Leave instructions for these letters to be distributed upon the event of your death. Part of grief is losing access to the person who's now gone—by leaving a letter of gratitude and shared remembrance for your loved ones, you could ease some of this pain and make sure that they know how much you loved them, which can be especially comforting if you happen to die unexpectedly. Even better—you could share your gratitude in person before you die so your loved one has no lingering doubts.

Legacy can also consist of material possessions. Some families put tags on heirlooms to specify their future owners. As an example: a mother asked all her children what heirlooms they wanted to keep, after she dies. She tagged furniture, clocks, tables and other precious items with their names. For jewelry and small things, she made a detailed list. For the things lots of her children wanted to keep, they drew straws. This approach to the division of your assets as part of your legacy reduces the risk of familial squabbling and can save headaches for the executor of your will.

Hildy's Story

In my family, one of my sisters wanted an unusual houseware, a pewter serving spoon. Three of my other siblings wanted a "Mighty Mine Dodgers" framed certificate, honoring my father for his submarine heroics during World War II. Another memento in hot demand was a carved statue of a lineman, a gift to my dad from a former employee. I wanted my mom's broken schoolhouse clock—which had sat in her kitchen when I was a child, and in our rumpus room when I was growing up. None of these things were worth a lot of money, but their association with my parents made them priceless. ⊛

Bright Idea

Think about what matters to you and how you want to be remembered. Leave a legacy by sharing what you've learned, to ensure your family and loved ones know how much you've loved them. If you can, remember not to leave things to the last minute—and never practice passive-aggressive behavior from beyond the grave. Ensuring a positive legacy for the next generation is something everyone can do with a little effort. It makes the lives of your loved ones better, and it helps the world in general—even if you're just making the lives in your corner of the world a little bit happier.

Ann's Story

My mother—who reluctantly adhered to the 50s idea that women should get married right after college, build a home, start a family and live happily-ever-after—had always resented the intellectual and social restrictions on her life. Initially delighted to see me embark upon a successful career and a happy marriage, her attitudes toward me changed dramatically when she found out I was pregnant, seeing that I could be a mother *and* have a career. Her yearning for the life that had been denied to her—all the while, witnessing *my* ability to do both— was an inadvertent cause of suffering for her, and created a tense mother-daughter dynamic between us. When she died, she asked my niece to distribute her jewelry. She gave her favorite daughter her wedding ring, another sister her watch, and a niece her beautiful pearls. I received an old, worn out jewelry bag, stained with makeup, filled with broken pieces of costume jewelry. While initially, I was stung with embarrassment and hurt that *this* was how my mother felt about me, I now see it as fitting metaphor for our broken relationship—stained with broken dreams, carried forward from the past. ⊛

This kind of behavior can also have unintended consequences for the favored siblings, not just the ones who feel left out or devalued. Jealousy and resentment over wills and decrees are a common storyline in movies and literature—because they happen all too often. A lingering feeling that "Mom or Dad loved you best" as shown by material value left in estate can irreparably damage lifelong family relationships. If you're ever tempted to go down this path— reconsider, remembering this quote:

> I've learned that people will
>
> Forget what you said,
>
> People will forget what you did
>
> But they will never forget how you made them feel.
>
> —*Maya Angelou*

Legacy Exercise

You can download Encore exercise from our website at https://yourencoreteam.com/. Use the legacy template to help you think about what you might want to leave behind.

Legacy

Life Long Learner

Curious

Ability to learn, understand, and appreciate others in a wide variety of environments and situations

Born with bright eyes and a creative spirit, survived challenging parents with the love and support of siblings, used my work to help heal myself, traveled the world to be a part of other ways of living, partnered with my husband to raise two wonderful women, and enJOYed a life well lived.

Your Skills *Your Story*

Ann's Sample Legacy exercise

Your Treasures *Your Wisdom*

Our Family

Nature

My journals

Friends and fun

Learning

Life

"The only true knowledge is self-knowledge." (Oscar Wilde)

We are here to work with the universe, discover our true nature, live life fully, and not fight these things on our journey.

Hildy's

Legacy

• Getting things done
• Instigating social events
• Can sign and remembers lyrics to 100's of songs
• Networking and sales of concepts
• Make a great Irish Scone

Middle child of a Irish Catholic family of seven who enjoyed a wonderful childhood with lovng parents and siblings. Married the love of my life Jim and had three lovely children and a fulfilling career in technology. Completely enjoyed the ride with friends and experiences I treasure.

Your Skills *Your Story*

Hildy's Sample Legacy exercise

Your Treasures *Your Wisdom*

• Brennan, Katie and Daniel
• Art collected from different anniversary trips around the world
• Siena Hill - our pastoral home in the SF Bay Area

"The secret of life is enjoying the passing of time, any fool can do it, there ain't nothing to it. Nobody knows how we got to the top of the hill, but since we're on our way down, might as well enjoy the ride" This song came along when I was in college and I always felt they were words to live by.

Chapter 12

Death

When you were born you cried,

And the world rejoiced.

Live your life so that when you die

The world cries and you rejoice.

—Navajo Chant

Denial of Death

In Ernest Becker's book, *The Denial of Death*, he talks about how our resistance to death shows up in American culture. Amassing huge fortunes, having statues made in our honor, and living "larger than life" all provide the illusion that somehow, we're the one special exception to the rule— but the truth is, no one gets out of here alive. Americans don't even like to mention the word *death*—we hide its messiness behind closed doors in hospitals, homes, and funeral parlors. The English language has more than 101 different euphemisms for the word death, on a spectrum ranging from distancing language ("awakened to eternal life") and sugar-coating it ("entered the sweet Hereafter") to the ironic ("checked into the Horizontal Hilton") and the macabre ("feeding the worms.")

Think about all the art created through the years to harness the life force, challenge the power of death, and plead for immortality. Consider the ubiquitous imagery of the *Ouroboros*. *Ouro* is Greek for tail, and boros is Greek for eating. The image of a snake eating its own tail— an image explored in depth by Joseph Campbell in his book *The Mythic Image*. The *Ouroboros* suggests the cycle of life and death over the millennia, a symbol associated with infinity and the

155

ever-present cycle of life and death we see in nature. Ancient people depicted the mystery of death in imagery so long ago—so why is it that we still struggle with the concept?

We look for ways to deny death by living life to its fullest. Candy Chang, author of *Before I Die* dealt with the grief of losing a dear friend by spontaneously writing,

Before I Die, I Want to _____ on the wall of an abandoned building in New Orleans. In just 24 hours, the wall had burst into life, full of specific aspirations, quickly going viral, recreated in over 500 cities and 70 countries. What a testament to the human need to proclaim our intentions for living life to the fullest!

Bright Idea

There are numerous websites with 100, 1000, even 10,000 things to do before you die, and there's also a movie called *The Bucket List*. Wikipedia even has a step-by-step tutorial for how to make your own bucket list! In one of his installations, artist Damien Hirst, who has a self-proclaimed "obsession with death," took a tiger shark, embalmed it, and suspended it in a tank so it simultaneously appears both alive and dead, titling it, *The Physical Impossibility of Death in the Mind of Someone Living*. Ironically, despite using over $100,000 worth of formaldehyde, the shark started to decompose, so a replacement shark had to be shipped in from Australia to replace the original. Being *human* means being *vulnerable*, with death representing the ultimate—and inescapable—vulnerability. This section of the book is to help you prepare for that eventuality, creating spaces for radical vulnerability to help guide you in preparation.

Death: The Final Frontier

As the days fly by—marked by special events like birthdays and other celebrations—have you ever wondered what will be your "death day?" Some lucky lives have a marvelous symmetry—coming into this world and then leaving in the same season. For example, a week before his birthday, singer Merle Haggard told his son that he would die on his 79th birthday—and then ful-filled his prediction. Was the statement a self-fulfilling prophecy, or was it his 6th sense kicking in, the realization that his body was preparing for the final transition? Many terminal people say that they can feel the telltale signs —it could be that our bodies give us signs of our impending death, but we may not be paying attention to these signs due to fear, or distracting ourselves from the inevitable.

Being able to contemplate your actual death is, at best, an abstraction. As George Bernard Shaw stated wryly, "Don't try to live forever, you won't succeed." Since it's impossible to guess at what death *feels like,* it's more useful to focus on the *ideal conditions* for your death. Some people want to die in their sleep, while others want to be fully conscious without the potential fuzziness of pain medication to say goodbye to loved ones. Just as each of us lives our lived in our own unique way, we'll each experience death in our own unique way.

Ann's Story

My dear friend Ginna—on vacation in Hawaii with her family—got the call from hospice that her mother was ready to die. After a challenging 16-hour trip to Portland, convinced she would arrive to find her moth-er already dead, she finally made it and was astonished her mother was still alive. To Ginna, it felt like her mother had *willed* herself to stay alive to see her beloved daughter one last time. Even though she was in a semi-comatose state, Ginna remains firm in the belief that she could listen to her grandchildren say good-bye to her on the speakerphone, and takes great comfort in knowing her mother died at peace—her way. ✹

Hildy's Story

My father served on a submarine in WWII. After the war, he vowed that he would see the *true millennium change* at the Royal Hawaiian Hotel where he'd been stationed during the war. As he approached New Year's Eve 2001, my father planned a family reunion in Hawaii. At this point, he was very ill, receiving blood transfusions three times a week in a losing battle with leukemia. It appeared that through sheer force of will he stayed alive to reach his goal of seeing in the new century in Hawaii. He died six months later. ❀

These stories point to a kind of premonition we each might possess about the timing of our death—as well as affirming that through sheer force of will, we sometimes get the closure we need. The theory of *willful dying*, indicates a divide in the genders, when it comes to death—the approach of a birthday or other sort of human marker of time can prolong life for a short time among women, but seems to hasten death among men, suggesting that birthdays serve as a "lifeline" for the women and a "deadline" for the men. Whether it's due to the comfort of friends, seeing something through to its completion, or being able to say goodbye to someone special— for some of us, the mind, body, and spirit appear to be work in unison to dictate the timing of your death.

The Institute of Medicine's definition of a **good death** is "...one that is free from avoidable distress and suffering, for patients, family, and caregivers; in general accord with the patients' and families' wishes; and reasonably consistent with clinical, cultural, and ethical standards." Patricia Wilson, the Executive Director of the Make-a-Wish Foundation, serving children with terminal diagnoses, believes there are 5 kinds of wishes she encounters consistently when a child is facing imminent death.

I wish to **go**

I wish to **be**

I wish to **meet**

I wish to **have**

I wish to **help**

Go— Be— Meet— Have — Help.

Children really do have all the answers, don't they? Children who've had to deal with very adult issues of pain, vulnerability, suffering, and the meaning of life want to know that they've made a positive impact on the world and those around them. Even as they confront their mortality, the wish to help others and leave the world a better place surfaces over and over again. Children facing death are more likely to live in the present, and want to understand how their life had meaning for others.

Ann's Story

At a Masters Swimming meet in California, a 65-year-old competitor suffered sudden cardiac arrest while swimming a distance race, was treated onsite and then transported to a local medical center, where he was pronounced dead on arrival. The athletes who remained at the meet were offered the option to move the remaining events to the following day or continue with the competition. People were shocked and upset, but considered carefully what to do next. They opted to continue after a moment of silence to honor the deceased participant—a striking example that the rivers of life forges on after you're gone, and for some of us, that continuation is the best respect you can pay to a life well-lived. ❀

Some people opt to plan their death—not entirely unlike they way you'd plan for a C-Section birth. At the time of this publication, resources are available in Vermont, Montana, Washington, New Mexico and Oregon for legally assisted dying, for people with terminal diagnoses. The

"Death with Dignity" movement actively advocates for changes to legislation that will empower terminally ill individuals to die in a peaceful, humane manner in the place and time of their choice. Contemporary research indicates that approximately 1 in 5 physicians have received a request for assisted death at some point in their medical practice, with 5-20% of such requests eventually honored in states where assisted dying is legal.

Creating a Death Plan

Have you considered creating a **Death Plan**? How do you want to spend your last days on this planet? Where do you want to be when you die? Dr. BJ Miller, former Director of Zen Hospice Center in San Francisco, is passionate about sharing the importance of active listening and honoring the unique needs of every person as they prepare to die, and whether their special requests have been recorded in a death plan. While Miller and his colleagues stress that no clinician can help to avert all of a person's suffering at the end of life, what they can offer is the simple practice of being present to witness the beauty, awe, and mystery of death by focusing deeply on the person. A "good death,"—much like a good birth—is witnessed by those with great love in their hearts and a support team who appreciates and can offer what's needed to best support the individual during their transition. The Zen Hospice Guest House is a small residential care facility in San Francisco serving the unique needs of people with less than six months to live who need a warm, supportive, family-like setting. Zen Hospice staff intentionally designed the environment of the Guest House for comfort, beauty, and sensory experiences delivered with tenderness—healthy, home cooked meals, the scent of fresh flowers from the garden floating in on fresh air.

Recently, we learned of death doulas who help to mentor the dying and their loved ones, to co-create peaceful exits. The International End of Life Doula Association offers training on techniques for converting compassion to specific practices that help those who're dying to connect in a meaningful way using rituals important to them with their family and friends. They've found that simple things are powerful and facilitate peace for both the person transitioning from life and those who're processing their loss. One doula shared the story of a man standing at the foot of the bed with the TV on, paralyzed with what to do as his mother lay dying. The doula encouraged him to turn off the television, come and hold her hand, and speak from the heart of what he appreciated about her, so her last moments were about connection, touch, and intimacy, enabling him to offer positive closure on a life well lived and to make him feel proud of the support he offered during this transition.

Like a birthing plan, creating a death plan can help capture more of the nuances around what you want. Wider-ranging than the **5 Wishes document**—which focuses on medical care, clinical treatment, and level of desired comfort or a checklist of medical interventions—creating your death plan lets your loved ones know the environment, rituals, and sensory elements you'd like to bring to death, if possible. It can help create a sense of calm to prepare for this final journey, with the added benefit of noticing and hopefully appreciating more deeply and consistently each day of health and happiness that comes before this time.

Ann's Story

The experience of writing my death plan was intense. While intellectually, it seemed like a good idea, it made me feel vulnerable, weak, and worried that I was hastening my own death by writing down my specific preferences. I started crying as I created it, and yet also felt strangely peaceful and grateful for the gift of life and the time I have left (which is hopefully a lot!). ✺

Bright Idea: Practice Dying

In yoga, one of the most emotionally challenging postures is called *shavasana*, or *corpse pose*. This posture is about totally releasing any tension in the mind or body without any movement whatsoever. Professor Robert Thurman, head of Tibetan Buddhist studies at Columbia University, notes that Buddhist monks practice their whole lives to be able practice the power of conscious dying. At the moment of death, the practitioner ejects their consciousness out of their body and into the clear light of wisdom. While we may not experience that exact same sensation, the act of preparing the mind, body, and spirit for death just as women prepare their mind, body, and spirit to give birth can empower us in ways we haven't considered. Like birth, death is a physical act that incorporates many of our senses, but while our parents often create their birth plan, we're responsible for creating our own death plan.

Ann's Death Plan

I'd like to be in my home, surrounded by my family. I'd like to be able to sit under a tree, or to be able to see the trees, birds, flowers, and sky so that I may deeply experience my connection to the people and beauty of nature, which have nurtured me throughout my life. I'd like to be comforted by touch by having my hand held, and if I'm able to, I'd like to eat my favorite foods—dark chocolate, avocado, strawberries, and a glass of red wine to toast to my life.

I hope my heart is full of gratitude, and that I feel at peace after a life well-lived and shared with those whom I love. I want to be conscious as I take my last breath, with a heart filled with a combined sense of relief and adventure to guide me into my final shavasana, and say one final thank you for having lived an incredible life.

Hildy's Death Plan

I'd like to be in my home—where a party is in progress. As an extrovert, I've always gained energy from engaging with people, and I'd hope my death would no different. Being Irish, I don't want to miss the wake! I want my closest friends and family to gather with me on my last day. I want to hear laughter and singing in the next room, as I hold court in my bedroom. One by one, I want the chance to visit with my loved ones and say goodbye. I hope to be well enough to express to each one what they've meant to me in my life, and to try to recall all the good times we've shared together—as well as to express why they've been important to me and what I wish for them. All my ducks will be in a row. I'll be ready to go, grateful for my life and curious about what's coming next.

Burial Plan

Consider what sociologist Kate Torgovnick May learned about burial rituals from other cultures: Torgovnik noted given the short supply of burial sites in South Korea, some enterprising companies offer an alternative to provide the ashes after cremation. They've figured out how to compress the remains into bead-like shapes that are then colorized for display in the relative's home—much like a piece of modern art. Maybe the Western world's new-found fondness for "green burials" was inspired by the Filipino Caviteno tribes, who have buried their dead in hollowed-out tree trunks for generations. In modernized "green burials," a biodegradable shroud may be used, with the body placed in a pine box, in a shallow grave no deeper than three feet to decompose. This not only saves money—it also prevents toxic embalming chemicals from further impacting our delicate environment. In Berlin, open space is at a premium, so some graveyards have been repurposed into playgrounds.

Many cultures implement intermediate steps before the disposal of the body. Consider, for example, the Irish tradition of wakes. Wakes precede the burial, with the body laid out in the parlor while the family holds a party, telling stories and toasting to the deceased. The origin of holding a wake is attributed to the Irish love of a good stout, served in a pewter mug. The combination of intoxication—combined with lead leaching from the goblet—is capable of creating a death-like stupor. Legend has it that after relocating the remains of loved ones only to discover scratch marks on the inside of coffins, some families decided to lay the body out to see if the person would suddenly "awake" before the burial. Hence, a popular ritual was created before burying the body—a little bit like the idea of being "saved by the bell."

Ann's Story

My friend Pauline and her family experienced both the joy of her eldest daughter's wedding celebration and the agony of learning that her son Mark had brain cancer—all within the space of the same week. Their entire family faced the challenges on his journey bravely and supported each other every step of the way. They honored his wishes for his death and memorial service, attended by over 400 people. Familial tensions increased when it came time to spread his ashes. While Pauline and her older daughter Ellen were ready, her younger daughter Mary was not. Each night, Pauline said *good night* to her son by looking up at the stars, thinking of him. Then, before a family trip to Hawaii, Mary was finally ready. A local florist in Hawaii made a unique floral covering for the water-soluble bag that contained his ashes. The family boated out at sunset—out on an unusually calm sea—to release him to the ocean, remembering all the fun times they'd had together boogie boarding on that beach. Upon their return to the condominium, Pauline's 7-year-old granddaughter said, "Gams, now you don't have to say goodnight to Mark." Finally, they were all at peace, having shared yet another beautiful memory of a beautiful human being. ✺

Memorial Service Plan

Planning your memorial isn't about you—not entirely, anyway. Your memorial is about helping your loved ones in their time of grief. Planning your memorial and documenting how you want your remains to be treated is one of the last acts of kindness you can perform for your loved ones. Planning beforehand will allow your friends and family to just grieve your loss—without the fear that they've somehow misinterpreted your wishes. Try to take into consideration the people you're leaving behind when you're planning your memorial or burial. What will *they* need to cope with your loss? Giving family members a role in your memorial or burial is one of many ways to invite the people you leave behind to show their love for you. Make plans for a reading, lighting a candle, singing a favorite song, preparing a video montage, or designating pallbearers are all ways you might include your loved ones in performing rituals that will help them to say goodbye. While it's easy to be glib, thinking, "None of that's my problem, after all, I'll be dead!" We urge you to consider a **Memorial Service Plan** as a final act of kindness for your loved ones. How do you envision your memorial service? Where would you want it held? Who would you like to attend it? What kind of music and speakers would you like, and how might you best prepare your instructions, so your loved ones aren't left to guess while they're grieving?

If religion or faith plays a part in your life, chances are some of the work will already be done for you. For most Christians, funeral services are generally held in churches, and involve readings and eulogies given by family, friends, and religious officiants. In many Jewish traditions, the body is buried within 24 hours of death with minimal or no embalming, while families sit *Shiva* for seven days in their home afterwards. Likewise, many Muslims also traditionally bury the body within 24 hours of death, and eschew embalming procedures, often opting for a simple shroud. For many Hindus, memorial services include the burning of body on a raft on open water, with grieving family on the banks in attendance. And those are just a few of the more commonly embraced religious approaches to funeral rites—there are multitudes of spiritual beliefs, traditions, and ceremonies specifically oriented to honor the dead and cherish the living, as we say goodbye to our loved ones.

If you don't ascribe to any specific religious traditions, you may still want to help your loved ones move on by conducting a *Celebration of Life* ceremony. As the name implies, Celebrations of Life are celebratory in nature, often conducted a few months following death, after people have had time to grieve properly. In their structure, Celebrations of Life can run the gamut: from a video tribute of the person's life set to music and good-natured "roasts" hosted by friends and family to dinner parties serving up a person's favorite meal—a Celebration of Life is a way to still "live on" in the present, even after you're gone.

Hildy's Story

My sister and I were on-point in preparing the memorial church service after my father's death. My mother selected his favorite hymns and my brother designed and printed the program. But none of us were prepared for the interview with the priest, because this was our first funeral. We did our best to appraise the priest on the highlights of dad's life, the things we thought he would want mentioned as part of his legacy. We told the priest about some of Dad's favorite activities—including his participation in the "Flying Fish" reunions of submariners from World War II, never once thinking that there might be another way that could be interpreted. Imagine our surprise when during the funeral mass, the priest wondered aloud at how happy my dad must be up in heaven fly-fishing. At first, we were all perplexed—Dad was definitely not an outdoorsman. My brother in-in-law later quipped, "If Dad was fly-fishing, he wasn't in heaven—he was in hell!" In retrospect, it might've helped if we'd been better prepared, or if we'd written down the most pertinent information for the priest, to help him with the eulogy. Even better—we could've asked Dad how he wanted to be remembered.

So unless you want to be accidentally eulogized as a fly-fisherman at your memorial (which is great, if you're a fly-fisherman!) creating a written death plan, deciding on your burial plan, and planning and formalizing your memorial are all final gifts that you can give to your loved ones.

No matter how much we prepare, death can still come as a surprise. The more you can prepare for this final transition the easier it'll be for your loved ones. ✹

Ann's Story

Both my mother-in-law and father-in-law lived well into their 90s, so my husband and his siblings have remained confident that they too will live into their 90s. After a meeting with his financial planner to modify their financial plans—with the assumption he would live to 100—after swimming one Sunday morning, my brother-in-law suffered a fatal cardiac event and was found dead in the hot tub at his gym.

Shocked and devastated to learn from a policeman knocking on her door to tell her the horrible news, that very day our sister-in-law was forced to make lots of decisions, guessing at what his wishes might've been for his memorial service, and the location of his internment—the only thing she knew for sure was that he didn't want to be cremated. She was devastated emotionally, and just wanted time to process and work through her feelings. The added stress of not knowing what else he wanted caused her a lot of wholly avoidable stress in an already-stressful time. Even if you feel confident about your health, it's still best to make these plans—just in case. ✹

 **Reflection**

Have you considered what you want for your memorial service?

_____

_____

_____

_____

_____

Do you have a burial plot selected or cremation place to scatter your ashes?

_____

_____

_____

_____

Who do you want to keep your ashes if you don't want them to be scattered?

_____

_____

_____

_____

_____

Have you talked to your loved ones about your specific wishes?

_____

_____

_____

_____

_____

_____

Chapter 13

Making It Real

Unceasing change turns the wheel of life, and so reality is shown in all its many forms. Dwell peacefully as change itself liberates all suffering sentient beings and brings them great joy.

—Amartya Sen

Y ou've given yourself a great gift by taking the time to explore what it means to live fully and firmly in the presence of death. Your journey may have been a linear path, with a logical progression though each chapter of this book—or it might've been a haphazard romp, with lots of meandering, stops, and starts. To recap and carry forward your learning, we're going to ask you the toughest question of all: **How do you make all of this real?**

By *real*, we mean converting your learning, intentions, and insights into *tangible outputs* you can return to in times of need, confusion, or in collaboration with your loved ones. The templates in the **Appendix** will make it easier to deal with whatever you find challenging. Whether it's creating an action plan to record all the loose ends you want to tie up, enlisting the support of an Accountability Buddy, or creating a Bucket List to capture all your passion and intentions in retirement, this's about synthesizing your learning in a way that's both meaningful and impactful for **YOU!**

Revisit the Wheel

Look at your "wheel of life" with fresh eyes. Redraw it here without looking at the first one you created. Now compare the two wheels.

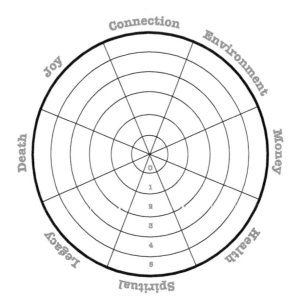

Refection

- What's changed on the wheel?
- How has it changed?
- Why has it changed?
- What's my Wheel of Life telling me today?
- What I am feeling about my Wheel of Life today?

Depending on your answers to the questions on the wheel, you might want to jump back to any given section in the book to explore that topic further. Did you look at all the resources provided? Did you fill out all the reflection questions for each section? A good way to check your preparedness is to print out our document inventory template from our website www.yourencoreteam.com and gather a copy of these documents into one folder for your executor or loved one. Let your executor and loved ones know where to find this important file. This's one of the kindest thoughtful acts you could do for your survivors, and could save them weeks and months of detective work.

Now that you've recorded your thoughts, feelings, and observations, you can luxuriate in the ability to re-read your reflections to look for patterns and identify insights.

Reflection

Do you notice any persistent themes in your answers?

_____

_____

_____

_____

Are you surprised at what you wrote, how you felt, or even how are you may have moved from your initial feelings and actions about this entire topic of retiring, dying and death?

_____

_____

_____

_____

Have you opted to share any of your reflections, and is there a bigger story waiting to be told or shared with a larger audience?

_____

_____

_____

_____

_____

_____

Reflections Review

Review your reflections and decide what action/s you will take in each area of your life. We recommend you use our **Life Stage** template to

record your top three insights and actions for every section of the wheel. Be sure to date the canvas. Plan on reviewing it as you age throughout this stage of your life—think of it as a living document. Your plans could change radically and could be out of your control. Unexpected illness, or inheritance could change how you approach this phase of your life.

Create and Share Your Life Stage

After reading this book, it's time for action. How might you convert your best intentions into reality? Creating a personalized action plan can be both a balm and a way to increase the likelihood you get your needs met and create a sense of calm for yourself and your loved ones. Some of us can create our **Life Stage** and then execute it, no problem. If that sounds like you, go for it!

Find an Accountability Buddy

Others of us need more support and structure, so having an **Accountability Buddy** can ensure our plan gets created—and completed! Consider who might be your Accountability Buddy. The logical buddy would be your life partner, but sometimes they may not be ready to consider their Encore just yet.

Requirements might include the following:

- Someone you know well and trust
- A spirit of reciprocity coupled with a sense of humor
- Common agreement about the "check-in" process and intervals on your plan

Once you've completed your respective plans, how will you celebrate? Ideas we've include cracking a special bottle of bubbly instead of "saving it for a special occasion," creating or purchasing a piece of art emblematic of the Circle of Life, or "paying it forward" by hosting a Death Café or becoming a Hospice volunteer. Remember—life is for the living and meant to be celebrated!

Moving beyond the **Life Stage**, is there anything you'd want to leave behind as a last act of love for your loved ones? Aside from financial and legal matters, is there a video you want to create, a letter you want to write, a poem to craft as a legacy that lives beyond you that might provide solace, deepen a bond made in life, or lighten the load of your loss? Would crafting your own eulogy or funeral service provide comfort to you, while alleviating a potential strain on your loved ones? Maybe you'd rather host your own Goodbye Party while you're still here—it's your party, you can cry if you want to!

Bright Idea

A young couple—devastated by the news that the wife had terminal cancer—decided to face this news by posting daily photographs of her as her illness progressed. They say a picture is worth a thousand words—these photographs served as a wordless photo essay, reflecting the fear, courage, beauty, devastation, love, and despair they shared through every step of the process. While many may shy away from such ideas, documenting your life before or during illness or death can serve as a comfort to you and as a reassurance to your loved ones. You can do this at any age, and if you choose to, consider the advice Socrates passed onto his followers as he lay dying, inviting them to practice dying as the highest form of wisdom. The more conscious you are of death, the more passionately you can embrace life.

Ann's Story

A dear friend of ours was diagnosed with pancreatic cancer but was *adamant* she was going to beat it. She didn't want any talk about death, despite dwindling to less than 90 pounds, losing control of her bowels, and becoming unable to leave her bed. She still insisted she was going to get better. She never talked to her teenage son about her illness or what was going on, and her amazingly dedicated and tenacious husband who'd been there for her every day was left to contend with guessing about what she wanted for her service. Many of us never got the chance to say goodbye to her, and our collective sense of sadness was intensified by our concern about the wellbeing of the family she left behind.

Through this, I learned the importance of thinking through the unintended consequences of being unable or unwilling to deal with the realities of death and the aftermath for your loved ones. I also learned about the common belief that positive thinking is always effective in beating illness and realized you can hold opposing beliefs simultaneously—*I'll be as positive as I can about overcoming my illness, and I need the peace of mind from taking care of the planning should I not be able to overcome my illness.*

It made me appreciate the power of taking care of loved ones, "from the grave," by making it easier for them to know how to structure the memorial service while coping with their own grief instead of trying to plan without any guidance. In watching my friend's son struggle to make sense of her death, I wondered if it might've been easier if she'd left a note, a video, or special book inscribed for him to remember her by. Her son is now in therapy, trying to make sense of his loss, her choices, and their connection. ✹

Document Inventory

Gather these important documents in one place and let your executor and loved ones know where to find it.   We have included some of the templates that were provided in this book and they are marked with an asterisk. You can download Encore exercises from our website at https://yourencoreteam.com/.

Joy

Do More/Less Bucket List*
Connection
Network of Support*
Environment
Purge, Protect & Optimize

Money

Important Information Inventory
Safety Deposit Box # & Key
Insurance Policies
Most recent Tax Return
Gift Tax Returns
Most recent W2
Mortgage Agreements
Title or Deeds to Any Property
Boats
Real Estate
Motor Vehicles
Year End Investment Statements
Health
Healthcare Power of Attorney
POLST form
Do not resuscitate (DNR)
Organ Donation plan
Health Calendar
Ask the Doctor

Spirituality

Dying Ritual

Death

Commemoration Plan
Will
Trust Documents
Power of Attorney
Cemetery / Funeral Arrangements
Legacy
Heart Map Bucket List
Letters to loved ones
Location and disposition of non financial treasures
Personal Information
Copy of Social Security card
Copy of passport
Armed Forces discharge papers
Birth certificate
Death certificates
Marriage certificate
Divorce certificate
Prenuptial agreements
Divorce settlements
Religious Affiliation

Chapter 14

Parting Thoughts

Parting thoughts on parting this world and the process of dying include great gratitude for the powerful team who helped us get our shared "labor of love" over the finish line. We would like to acknowledge Allie Marini for her enthusiasm, editorial expertise, and patience with us and the numerous renditions of our "final" text and Karen Bauermeister for her gentle spirit and creative talent in highlighting our words with beautiful images and converting our draft to a compelling book format. We also acknowledge our spouses, Jim DeFrisco and Steve Bundy, as well as our respective family members for encouraging us, supporting us, and celebrating our mini-milestones with delectable Manhattans!

We are also very grateful to you, our fellow life travelers, for your interest in and focus on this final part of life. Our mission in writing this book was to help open minds, initiate dialogue, and spark awareness of and reflection on the final frontier—death. By offering tools, ideas, and resources, we hope that you'll be able to assess where you are, reflect on your remaining years of living, and plan where you're going with grace and confidence in the transitions we talk about the least. We hope we've helped you redirect any fears about retirement and aging into positive energy for living in the now!

Finishing this book is yet another mini-ending—another chance for to practice with greater awareness and appreciation for the process that Swiss-American psychiatrist Elisabeth Kübler-

Ross introduced to help people understand the natural processes we go through during times of transition, death, and change through the theory of the **Five Stages of Grief**, which we've included in the **Digital Resource PDF**. We're confident that using the **Wheel of Life** to examine where you are on planning and executing this stage of your life will empower you to make choices that are right for you. Our wish is that our readers and social community are never stuck in the "pit of despair" represented in the Kübler-Ross Change Curve.

By educating yourself on your options, you can escape the denial trap that lurks in this last stage of life. Consider the words of wisdom from guru Thich Nhat Hanh on Embracing Reality, Five Remembrances:

When you deny the reality of life, you appreciate it less.

Meditate on the Buddha's Five Remembrances and rediscover the magic of life just as it is.

> *I am of the nature to grow old.*
>
> *There is no way to escape growing old.*
>
> *I am of the nature to have ill health.*
>
> *There is no way to escape ill health.*
>
> *I am of the nature to die.*
>
> *There is no way to escape death.*
>
> *All that is dear to me and everyone I love*
>
> *are the nature to change.*
>
> *There is no way to escape*
>
> *being separated from them.*
>
> *My actions are my only true belongings.*
>
> *I cannot escape the consequences of my actions.*
>
> *My actions are the ground upon which I stand.*

Bright Idea

What has the experience been for you in using this book as a tool for your own process of discovery? We want to hear your story, your thoughts, and your input. We'd like to welcome you to join the conversation on our website, www.yourencoreteam.com. Indulge yourself by listening to others' stories as well. Feel free to post either an auditory recording or video of your story on our website: www.yourencoreteam.com. We look forward to sharing your experiences!

Appendix

Document Inventory

Gather these important documents in one place and let your executor and loved ones know where to find it.

Joy

- Do More/Less Bucket List

Connection

- Network of Support

Environment

- Purge, Protect & Optimize

Money

- Important Information Inventory
- Safety Deposit Box # & Key
- Insurance Policies
- Most recent Tax Return
- Gift Tax Returns
- Most recent W2
- Mortgage Agreements
- Title or Deeds to any:
- Property
- Boats
- Real Estate
- Motor Vehicles
- Year End Investment Statements

Health
- Healthcare Power of Attorney
- POLST form
- Not resuscitate form (DNR)
- Organ Donation plan
- My Health Plan
- Health Calendar
- Ask the Doctor

Spirituality
- Dying Ritual

Death
- Commemoration Plan
- Will
- Trust Documents
- Power of Attorney
- Cemetery / Funeral Arrangements

Legacy
- Heart Map Bucket List
- Letters to loved ones
- Location and disposition of non-financial treasures

Personal Information
- Copy of Social Security card
- Copy of passport
- Armed Forces discharge papers
- Birth certificate
- Death certificates
- Marriage certificate
- Divorce certificate
- Prenuptial agreements
- Divorce settlements
- Religious Affiliation

Resistance-O-Meter

You: Plot a Triangle

Significant Others: Plot Diamonds

Your Parents: Plot Squares

Your Children: Plot Hearts

No Discussion   Freely Discuss Death

No Discussion   Freely Discuss Death

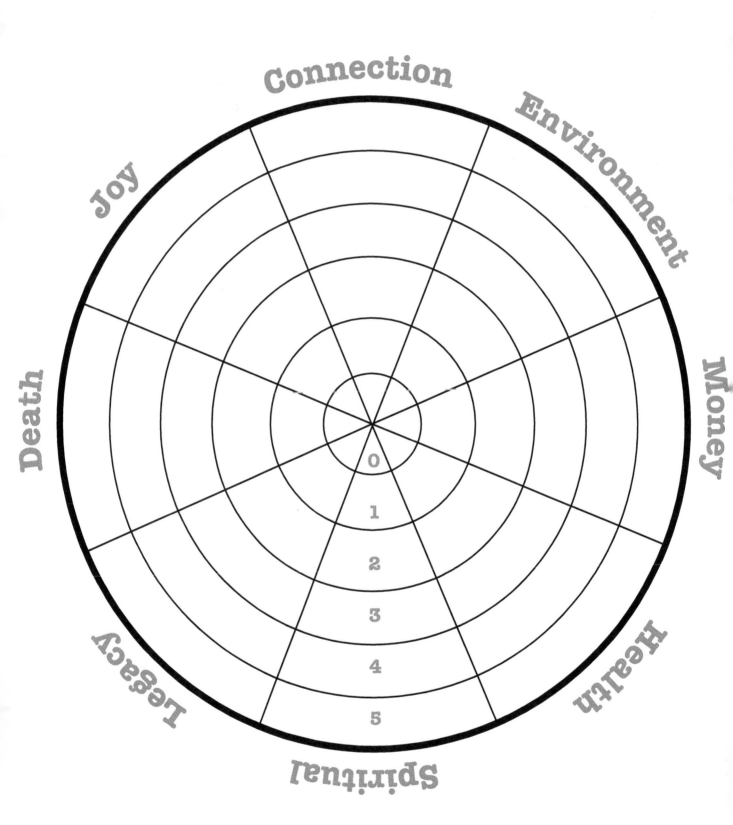

Date:_____

_____

_____

_____

_____

_____

Date:_____

_____

_____

_____

_____

_____

Date:_____

_____

_____

_____

_____

_____

Date:_____

_____

_____

_____

_____

_____

| Joy | Connections | Health | Spirituality | Legacy |

Environment

Death

Money

Bright Ideas

Stage Left   Center Stage   Stage Left

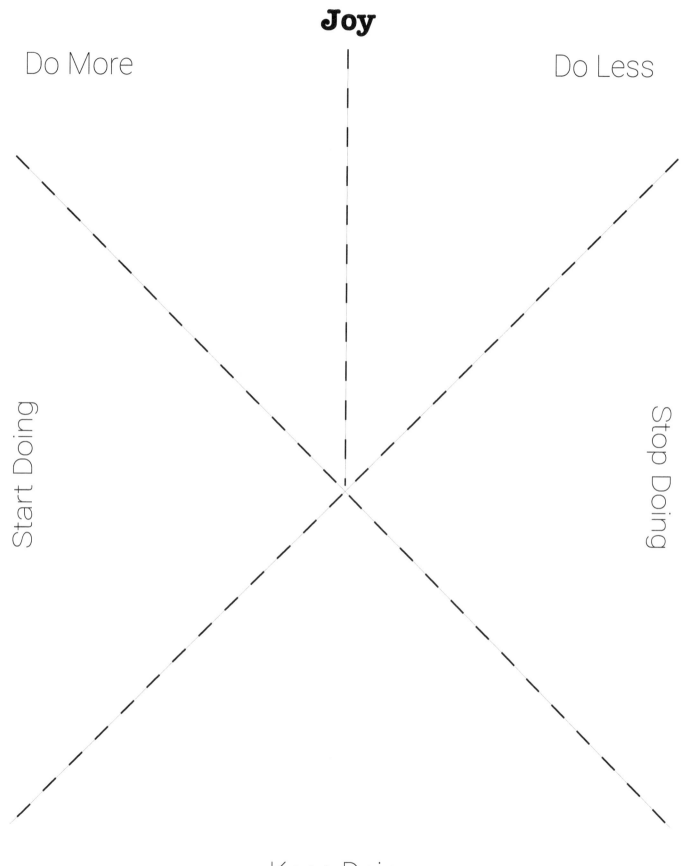

Optimize Your Environment

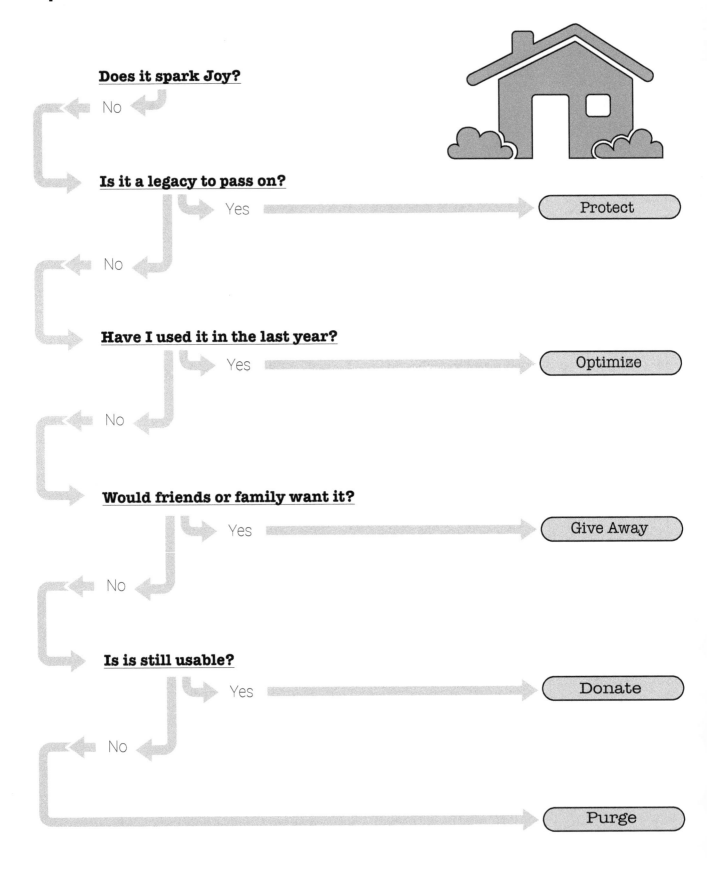

Does it spark Joy?

No

Is it a legacy to pass on?

Yes → Protect

No

Have I used it in the last year?

Yes → Optimize

No

Would friends or family want it?

Yes → Give Away

No

Is is still usable?

Yes → Donate

No → Purge

Healthcare Year at a Glance

Practice	Jan	Feb	Mar	Apr	May	June	Jul	Aug	Sep	Oct	Nov	Dec
Primary Care												
Dentist												
Eye Doctor												
Dermatologist												
Audiologist												
Physical Therapist												
Chiropractor												
Cardiologist												
Orthopedist												
Neurologist												

Dying Rituals

What comforted you as a child?

_____
_____
_____
_____
_____
_____

What sensory additions do you prefer?

_____
_____
_____
_____
_____
_____

What nourishes you now?

_____
_____
_____
_____
_____
_____

Are there family traditions you could use?

_____
_____
_____
_____
_____
_____

Legacy

Your Skills

Your Story

Your Treasures

Your Wisdom

Works Cited

AAFP. *SORT: The Strength-of-Recommendation Taxonomy. American Family Physician*, https://www.aafp.org/dam/AAFP/documents/journals/afp/sortdef07.pdf. Accessed 28 Jan. 2019

AARP Research & Strategic Analysis. *Beyond Happiness: Thriving*. AARP, June 2012, http://www.aarp.org/research/topics/life/info-2014/happiness-report-2012.html. Accessed 28 Jan. 2019

Adventist University of Health Sciences. *5 Characteristics of a Successful Nurse*. ADU, 2017, https://online.adu.edu/blog/all/articles/5-characteristics-of-a-successful-nurse/

https://online.ahu.edu/resources/blog/. 28 Jan. 2019

Alarcon, Renato D. *Global Mental Health and the Demolition of Culture*. Psychiatric Times, 27 Sept. 2016

http://www.psychiatrictimes.com/cultural-psychiatry/global-mental-health-and- demolition-culture. Accessed 28 Jan. 2019

Allaniz Study. *Women, Money, and Power*. Allaniz, 2013,

https://www.allianzlife.com/- /media/files/allianz/documents/ent_1462_n.pdf?la=en&hash=DB76F6EE3B711B77523A ABC237F9B37F6E8F2F21. 28 Jan. 2019

Anderson, Megory. *Sacred Dying, Creating Rituals for Embracing the End of Life*

Massachusetts, Da capo lifelong books, 2003

Barnes-Holmes, D and Hughes S. A Functional Approach to the Study of Human Emotion: The Centrality of Relational/Propositional Processes. In D. Hermans, B. Rimé, & B. Mesquita, (Eds). *Changing Emotions*. Psychology Press, 2013

Becker, Earnest. *The Denial of Death*. Michigan, Free Press, 1973

Brethauer, Erin, and Hussin Tim. *Secret speakeasy offers a window into San Francisco's past*. San Fransico Chnronicles, 26 March 2016, https://www.sfchronicle.com/the-take/article/Secret-speakeasy-offers-a-window-into-San- 7959969.php. Accessed 28 Jan. 2019

Brodsky, Matthew. *Best Long Term Care Insurance Companies*. Consumer Affairs, 11 July 2017, http://www.consumeraffairs.com/insurance/ltc.html. Accessed 28 Jan. 2019

Campbell, Joseph. *The Mythic Image*. New Jersey, Princeton University Press, 1981

Chaffey, Dave. *Global Social Media Research Summary 2018*. Smart Insights, 23 Nov. 2018, http://www.smartinsights.com/social-media-marketing/social-media-strategy/new-global-social-media-research/ for both statistics. Accessed 28 Jan. 2019

Chang, Candy. *Before I die*. New York, St. Martin's Griffin, 2013

Chatzy, Jean. *Here's the biggest fear women have about money*. Today, 18 July 2016, https://www.today.com/money/here-s-biggest-fear-women-have-about-money-t100865. Accessed 28 Jan. 2019

Curtiss, Karen. *Safe and Sound in the Hospital : Must-Have Checklists for Getting the Care You Want for the People You Love*. Minnesota, PartnerHealth, 2011

Dying Consciously. *Ceremony and Ritual*. Dying Consciously, 2016, http://www.dyingconsciously.org/ceremony-and-ritual/. Accessed 28 Jan. 2019

Fischer, Norman. *Sailing Home: Using the Wisdom of Homer's Odyssey to Navigate Life's Perils and Pitfalls*.Berkely, North Atlantic Books, 2011

Friedman, Richard A. *Fast Time and the Aging Mind*. The New York Times, 20 July 2013, https://www.nytimes.com/2013/07/21/opinion/sunday/fast-time-and-the-aging-mind.html. Accessed 28 Jan. 2019

Gannon, Sharon. *Closing the Gates*. Yoga Studio, 1 Jan. 2012, http://yogastudioofcc.com/tag/sharon-gannon/page/2/. Accessed 28 Jan. 2019

Glamping Hub. *Explore Wildly*. Glamping Hub, 2018, https://glampinghub.com/. Accessed 28 Jan. 2019

Golson, Jordan. *Volkswagen's Electric Bus Concept is a Groovy, Far Out Vision for the Future*. The Verge, 5 Jan. 2016, https://www.theverge.com/2016/1/5/10719412/volkswagen- budd-e-concept-car-electric-microbus-ces-2016. Accessed 28 Jan. 2019

Gustafson, David H. "A good death" *Journal of medical Internet research* vol. 9,1 e6. 14 Mar. 2007, doi:10.2196/jmir.9.1.e6

Hirst, Damien. *The Physical Impossibility of Death in the Mind of Someone Living*. Wikipedia, 7 Jan. 2017 https://en.wikipedia.org/wiki/The_Physical_Impossibility_of_Death_in_the_Mind_of_So meone_Living. Accessed 28 Jan. 2019

Hogan, Micheal. *Love at Any Age*. Psychology Today, 11 Feb. 2013, https://www.psychologytoday.com/blog/in-one-lifespan/201302/love-any-age. Accessed 28 Jan. 2019

Insured Retired Institute. *Newsroom Detail View*. IRV, 2017, http://irionline.org/newsroom/ newsroom-detail-view/boomers-confidence-in-secure- retirement-sinks-to-five-year-low. Accessed 28 Jan. 2019

Fries, James F. "Aging, Natural Death, and the Compression of Morbidity." *The New England Journal of Medicine*, vol. 80 (1980): 130- 247

Institute of Economic Affairs. *Retirement causes a major decline in physical and mental health, new research finds.* IEA, 16 May 2013, https://iea.org.uk/in-the-media/press-release/retirement- causes-a-major-decline-in-physical-and-mental-health-new-re-sea. Accessed 28 Jan. 2019

Jansen, Tiffany R. *The Preschool inside a Nursing Home.* The Atlantic, 20 Jan. 2016. http://www.theatlantic.com/education/archive/2016/01/the-preschool-inside-a-nursing- home/424827/. Accessed 28 Jan. 2019

Jobs, Steve. *How to Live before you die.* Ted, June 2005, https://www.ted.com/talks/ steve_jobs_how_to_live_before_you_die. Accessed 28 Jan. 2019

Kate, Roiphe. *The Violet Hour: Great Writers at the End.* New York,The Dial Press, 2016

Kerley, Deanna. 100 Pieces of Advice from 100 Year Olds. Mental Floss, 8 Aug. 2015, http://mentalfloss.com/article/54286/100-pieces-advice-100-year-olds. Accessed 28 Jan. 2019

Kim, Sung-Eun et al. "Sex- and gender-specific disparities in colorectal cancer risk" *World Journal of Gastroenterology* vol. 21,17 (2015): 5167-75.

Kokuamau. *The Last Stages of Life.* Kokua Mau, http://kokuamau.org/resources/last-stages-life. Accessed 28 Jan. 2019

Kübler-Ross, Elisabeth. *On Death and Dying.* New York, Scribner, 2011

Lang, Marissa. *As Employees Care for Aging Parents, Few Firms Step Up to Help.* SF Chronicle, 23 Sept 2016, http://www.sfchronicle.com/business/article/As-employ-ees- care-for-aging-parents-companies-9242430.php Accessed 28 Jan. 2019

Lawrence, Samuel. *Can We Die Naturally When We Choose?* Psychology Today, 13 Jan. 2014, https://www.psychologytoday.com/intl/blog/psychology-yesterday/201401/ can-we-die- naturally-when-we-choose. Accessed 28 Jan. 2019

Levine, Steve. *A Year to Live: How to Live This Year as If It Were Your Last*. New York, Bell Tower, 1998

Livingston, Gretchen. *Four in Ten Couples Are Saying I Do Again*. Pew Research Center, 14 Nov. 2014, http://www.pewsocialtrends.org/2014/11/14/four-in-ten-couples-are-saying-i- do-again/#remarriage Accessed 28 Jan. 2019

Lundy, Karen Saucier, and Sharyn James. *Community Health Nursing: Caring for the Public's Health*. Massachusetts, Jones and Bartlett Publishers, 2009.

McClellan, Martha. *The Aging Athlete: What We Do to Stay in the Game*. Self Publisher, 2014

Melnick, Meredith. *The Age-Defying Benefits of Having Older (And Younger) Friends*. Huffington Post, 5 June 2014, https://www.huffingtonpost.com/2014/05/06/heres-why-you-should-seek_n_5120705.html. Accessed 28 Jan. 2019

Miller, Shelley. *8 Easy Ways to Choose a Home Swap Club and Enjoy a Dream Vacation for Half the Price*. Huffington Post. 9 April 2013, https://www.huffpost.com/entry/8-easy- ways-to-choose-a-h_b_2593116. Accessed 28 Jan. 2019

Morris, Nathaniel P. *Mental illness and heart disease are often found in the same patients*. The Washington Post, 18 Feb. 2017, https://www.washingtonpost.com/national/health- science/mental-illness-and-heart-disease-are-often-found-in-the-same- patients/2017/02/17/665e5dd0-ee1d-11e6-9973- c5efb7ccfb0d_story.html?utm_term=.89bf42fc5525. Accessed 28 Jan. 2019

National Alliance on Mental Illness (NAMI). *Mental Health by the Numbers*. NAMI, 2015 http://www.nami.org/Learn-More/Mental-Health-By-the-Numbers. Accessed 28 Jan. 2019

Northrup, Christiane. *Goddesses Never Age: The Secret Prescription for Radiance, Vitality, and Well-Being*. California, Hay House Inc., 2015.

Pychyal, Timothy A. *Solving the Procrastination Puzzle: A Concise Guide to Strategies for Change*. Penguin, 2013

Raymond, Chris. *Euphemisms for Dead, Death, and Dying: Are They Helpful or Harmful?*. Very Well, 18 Aug. 2016, https://www.verywell.com/euphemisms-for-dead-death-or-dying- 1131903. Accessed 28 Jan. 2019

Reed, Carey. *Dutch Nursing Home Offers Rent-Free Housing to Students.* PBS, 5 April 2015, http://www.pbs.org/newshour/rundown/dutch-retirement-home-offers-rent-free-housing- students-one-condition/ . Accessed 28 Jan. 2019

Reyes, AG. *The Ultimate USA Wonders List.* List Challenges, 2019 http://www.listchalleng-es.com/the-ultimate-usa-wonders-list. Accessed 28 Jan. 2019

Sheehy, Gail. *Passages: Predictable Crises of Adult Life.* New York, Bantam, 1977

Shin, Laura. *The Money Taboo: Why It Exists, Who It Benefits, and How to Navigate It.* Forbes, 14 April 2015, https://www.forbes.com/sites/laurashin/2015/04/14/the-money-taboo- why-it-exists-who-it-benefits-and-how-to-navigate-it/#-5c62ad392f62. Accessed 28 Jan. 2019

Silverstein, Shel. *Giving Tree.* New York, HarperCollins, 1999

Stanford Medicine. *Death and Dying in the United States.* Palliative Care, 2019, https://palliative.stanford.edu/overview-of-palliative-care/death-and-dying-in-the-united-states/. Accessed 28 Jan. 2019

Steinberg, Steven M. "Cultural and religious aspects of palliative care"*International journal of critical illness and injury science* vol. 1,2 (2011): 154-6

Teno, Joan M et al. "Change in end-of-life care for Medicare beneficiaries: site of death, place of care, and health care transitions in 2000, 2005, and 2009"*JAMA* vol. 309, 5 (2013): 470- 7

Today. *Pauley: 'I was suffering from bipolar disorder'.* Today, 30 Aug. 2004, http://www.today.com/popculture/pauley-i-was-suffering-bipolar-disorder-2D80555775. Accessed 28 Jan. 2019

Tolle, Eckhart. *The Power of Now: A guide to Spiritual Enlightenment.* Carlifonia, New World Library Headquaters, 2004

Torgovnick, Kate. *Death is not the end: Fascinating funeral traditions from around the globe.* Ideas Ted, 1 Oct. 2013, http://ideas.ted.com/11-fascinating-funeral-tradi-tions-from- around-the-globe/. Accessed 28 Jan. 2019

Vark. *Vark: A Guide to Learning Styles.* Vark, 2019, http://vark-learn.com/. Accessed 28 Jan. 2019

Wikihow. *How to Open Your Spiritual Chakras.* Wikihow, http://www.wikihow.com/Open-Your-Spiritual-Chakras. Accessed 28 Jan. 2019

Wikipedia. *Observer Effect Definition*. Wikipedia, https://en.wikipedia.org/wiki/Observer_effect_(physics). Accessed 28 Jan. 2019

World Justice Project. *Join us at World Justice Forum VI*. World Justice Project, 2017,

https://worldjusticeproject.org/. Accessed 28 Jan. 2019

Zackheim, Victoria. *Exit Laughing: How Humor Takes the Sting Out of Death*. California, North Atlantic Books, 2012

Zelinski, Ernie. *How to Retire Happy, Wild, and Free: Retirement Wisdom That You Won't Get from Your Financial Advisor*. Essex, Visions International Publishing, 2013

Zen Hospice Project. *Who we are*. Zen Hospice, 2019, https://www.zenhospice.org/about/ Accessed 28 Jan. 2019

CPSIA information can be obtained
at www.ICGtesting.com
Printed in the USA
LVHW022139300620
659360LV00014B/613